Jerome Bert~

WALKING WITH GOD

The Story of a Pilgrimage
and the Spiritual Life

FAMILY PUBLICATIONS • OXFORD

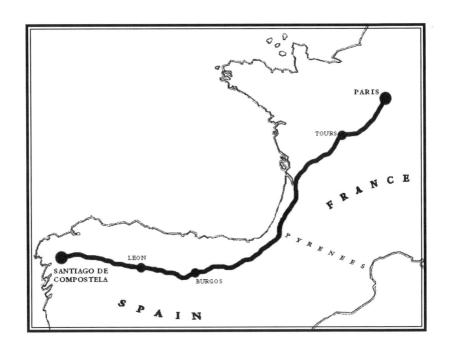

"...and Enoch walked with God and was not."

D. *Antonium Mª Romo Varela*

hujus Almae Apostolicae et Metropolitanae Ecclesiae Compos-
tellanae Dignitas Decani et sigilli Altaris Beati Jacobi Apostoli
custos, ut omnibus Fidelibus et Peregrinis ex toto terrarum
Orbe, devotionis affectu vel voti causa, ad limina Apostoli
Nostri Hispaniarum Patroni ac Tutelaris **SANCTI JACOBI**
convenientibus, authenticas visitationis litteras expediat, omnibus et singulis praesentes inspecturis, notum facio: *Dm*
Jerónimum Bertrán
hoc sacratissimum Templum pietatis causa devote visitasse.
In quorum fidem praesentes litteras, nomine meo subscriptas
et sigilo ejusdem Sanctae Ecclesiae munitas, ei confero.
    Datum Compostellae die **26** mensis *Augusti*
anno Dñi **1983**.-

© Family Publications 2006
All rights reserved

ISBN 1-871217-62-8

Front Cover Picture: J Bertram
Back Cover Picture: V Easterbrook

Published by

Family Publications
6a King Street, Oxford, OX2 6DF
www.familypublications.co.uk

Printed in England by
Cromwell Press, Trowbridge

Contents

Foreword

In preparing these pages for publication I have been revisiting memories of twenty years ago and more: it was in 1983 that we walked to Compostela, and it was 1988 when I was challenged by the Carmelite sisters of Chichester to preach their annual retreat. They required fifteen conferences: a structure naturally suggested itself, and my reflections on the three stages of our pilgrimage gave me ideas for illustrating the theme of a journey in prayer. So it came to pass. The good nuns (to my horror) tape-recorded the conferences, and Brenda Keats, parish secretary in Sutton Park, heroically undertook to transcribe the tapes to an Amstrad word-processor. A few copies were run off, but it is only now that they are being properly published.

Now the spoken word, however much people may claim to appreciate it at the time, doesn't read very well on paper, but I baulked at recasting the whole thing as a completely new book, so here you have more or less the words as spoken, but tidied up and (I hope) improved a bit. Maybe I would put it slightly differently now, but I think that what I said all those years ago is still valid, for lay readers as for religious. In fact it was lay readers of the first samizdat edition (a collector's item, surely) who were the most appreciative, which shows that prayer is not the preserve of the professionals, but is the privilege of every baptised Christian.

Not much else is still the same. Of the companions who walked with me to Santiago, nearly all have lost touch. Some did try their vocations to the priesthood or religious life, but it didn't work out for them. Some are happily married, one at least a member of an apostolic lay institute. It is part of the mission of the priest to get to know people, help them on their way a little, and then move on. You and they move in different directions, and our paths may not cross again until the Last Day when there will be uncounted reunions and recognitions. Tragically the Carmelites have dispersed from Chichester; they never fell away from their vocation of prayer for the world, but were unable to recruit new members, and left in the early 1990s. Their choir grille, through which I delivered the retreat conferences, now screens the relic chapel in the Oxford Oratory; here many of the relics which had been treasured at Chichester, and at Hoogstraat before that, have found a home. And, for that matter, so have I. The Amstrad also is no more, and the glorious Locoscript word-processing package which served so well has had to yield to much inferior mass-market programs. But in its dying days the old Amstrad was able selflessly to translate the files, so that Brenda's typing has survived the change of era.

To my students at London University, my parishioners at Sutton Park, the sisters of Carmel, and my fellow priests including one who actually stayed at Carmel with me for the first days of the retreat, the message is still walk in joy, persevere through the dark days, and rejoice in glory at the world's end!

J.F.A.B., Oxford 2006.

To Begin With

Since the pages that follow were originally delivered during a retreat to the Carmelite sisters, many of my comments about prayer and the Christian life were given in an enclosed religious context, which might make seculars wonder whether any of it is relevant to them. Yet I have to confess to being a secular myself: at the time the retreat was given I had been working for six years as a University chaplain, and my experience was in directing and being directed in the search for prayer in a secular, that is ordinary worldly, environment. Which means that probably (for I can only hope) what I have to say about prayer will be of some use or interest to layfolk and secular clergy rather than only to enclosed Religious. Indeed it seems rather cheeky for a secular priest to dare to talk to Carmelites about prayer at all: I should be much more at ease with a non-professional lay audience!

A retreat, naturally, is quite different from a study course or an academic conference. A retreat is a time to think about things we already know, not to learn new things. I can even express a hope that I'm not going to say anything that you don't already know perfectly well: my task is to remind you of things you might have wanted to forget, and to encourage you to continue on your pilgrimage, whatever comes. Similarly our daily prayer time, like a retreat, is a time to be quiet with God: not a time for intellectual activity, not a time for theology and certainly not a time for philosophy. It's a time to be quiet with God. The Gospels tell us of the time when the disciples were so pressed by the crowd, by people thronging with diseases to be cured, loaves to be multiplied and mothers-in-law to be healed, that there was no time for them even to eat. So Our Lord said "Come away to a quiet place where we can be by ourselves and rest there." Many times we read that Our Lord slipped away on his own to a desert place to pray. After that hectic day described at the opening of St Mark's Gospel the disciples collapsed into bed, and it was only when they woke in the morning that they wondered where Jesus was – and they found that he'd been out in the desert all night, praying.

It is a natural and sound instinct to escape into the desert to try and find somewhere quiet to be with God. Elijah, John the Baptist, the hermits who were the original Carmelites, all made a point of finding somewhere quiet. But the difficulty is that, wherever we are in this world, whenever we think we have found a quiet place, we become aware of noise. There is nowhere quiet in this country: even on top of the hills, the Downs or the Pennines, you will be able to hear a tractor somewhere in the background, or perhaps a nightingale singing or even a raven quothing. Why even within Carmel you can hear aeroplanes going overhead, to say nothing of the noises made by the community! The squeak of wheelchairs on polished floors can be very penetrating.

There are distractions and noises wherever we are, and we must be careful to avoid the trap of trying to go further and further into the desert, searching for an escape. If you read the lives of the Desert Fathers you find that to begin with they just settled in Lower Egypt like everybody else. Then they found that the noise of all the other hermits was more than they could stand, so they fled into Upper Egypt, further and further away from human contact. But even there they found continual interruptions, as you might expect. The old legends tell us of all the wild animals that appeared, often in amusing ways: lions volunteered to do the shopping, stags took refuge from robbers, flies acted as bookmarkers. To judge from the stories, being a hermit in the desert was one distraction after another. Certainly St Jerome tried it and had to give up in disgust after a few months. There is no silence in the desert.

I am talking about the search for silence, because of all the senses hearing is the most intrusive. Other senses can be equally distracting, but they are easier to cut out. We can avoid distracting sights by just closing our eyes, but there doesn't seem to be any way of closing our ears. So if we are looking for total silence we usually end up totally distracted. Imagine yourself in a deep cave, far underground: a place, you might think, of total silence, of total darkness where nothing could stop us praying ... but listen: somewhere far away there is a drip of water, some soft sound as of a slimy creature slithering over the stones towards us. There are terrifying glimpses of faint light that conceal some nameless dread.... No, deep caverns are not conducive to prayer! We're just as distracted as ever.

Even if you could find a perfect cell, somewhere absolutely quiet with no distractions at all, somewhere with no sights to allure us, no cobwebs begging us to get up and dust them, no lingering smells of onions left over from last night's cooking, no enticing touch or taste or anything, even there we wouldn't be able to listen to God because we bring all our own distractions with us and our minds would be teeming with remembered sights, sounds and smells, touches and so on, until we are right back where we started from. That is what the Desert Fathers all found as well: if there was a moment's peace and quiet outside, they found themselves tormented by devils, all the memories and temptations of their whole previous life bubbling up inside. You can't get away from distractions.

And so we really have to start all over again. Instead of hoping for a silence outside us we have to look for a silence inside. That's where we have to be in a retreat: in an interior cell, an interior desert. Now a remarkable thing, learned through the experience of centuries, is that often the best way to find silence inside is to make some sort of friendly noise outside. Even unbelievers have discovered that: if you run a noisy factory you put on music to calm down the workers, so that the sound of the music covers up the distracting noise of the machinery. You can override internal distractions with various sorts of regular rhythmic sound. That is the origin of the whole tradition of church music. You can't escape from distracting noises and thoughts, but you can cover them with a noise that doesn't distract but tells us about God. That's the particular benefit of chanting the psalms: the regular plainsong melody, the words of the psalms, the music of the accompaniment, actually become means to interior silence.

This is something the wisdom of ages has always known, and the Church managed to forget in the 1960s. Now we are rediscovering it. The chant, the rhythm and the sound of the words mean much more than the text. We can remember that when we sing our Office, or even if we only say it. If we actually attended to the textual meaning of every one of the psalms, there is far too much to take in. Even in the Little Hours we have three psalms, a short reading, a hymn and a prayer; and if you really thought about the meaning of every single word in the shortest Little Hour, you would have enough intellectual stimulation for years of study. I think it would be humanly impossible to be attentive to the meaning of every word, all the way through the Divine Office. That is why what we actually do is to attend more to the sound and the rhythm, the metre of the verse. We can feel the metre coming across as we recite the psalms, and the pulse of the music if we're singing. It is the sound that actually stills us inside, so that out of all those words perhaps one phrase, one sentence at most, can claim its place. Today we might notice the third verse of the second psalm; perhaps next time that Office comes round we can attend to the fourth verse. After fifty years of reciting the Office, every verse of every psalm will have had its chance to speak to us. It can do so because we've allowed the sound of the psalms to make us quiet inside.

If we are afraid of distraction by the senses, the way to attend to God is not so much to let them distract us, as attract us. That is the function not only of sacred music, but of sacred art, all the trappings and trimmings of the Liturgy. All these things were designed to make us quiet inside: something which tragically we seem to have forgotten. The Puritans in the sixteenth century attempted to get rid of all these things like music and colour and religious art, and make everything absolutely plain. Absurdly, Catholics made exactly the same mistake in the 1960s. They were trying, you see, to find somewhere like the ideal cell where there are no distractions; and, just as the desert fathers found, when you have a liturgy, a form of prayer, that is completely stark, all the distractions come crowding in again, and you no longer have any way to get rid of them.

That's why in the wisdom of the Church we are now rediscovering the sacred chant and the glory of the liturgy. That's something which was never lost in Carmel, and I'm always glad when I visit here to see how beautifully the altar is prepared. The sanctuary has never been stripped, made bare and stark and grey, as alas in some convents and many parish churches it has been. When I come to Carmel the altar linen is always immaculate. It reminds me of how St Teresa was once rebuked by St John of the Cross for providing scented rose water at the lavabo: "But of course," she said, "everything must be of the best for the altar of the Lord." It is nice to find everything clean and fresh on the sanctuary in Carmel: if only it were the same in all other churches!

Things of beauty speak to us through the senses, and these can really become ways to make us quieter and more attentive to God inside. The beauty of the chant is something that makes it possible to be quiet within ourselves. The beauty of sacred art has the same purpose: look at the statue of Our Lady, or the altar, the images, the Crucifix, best of all the Blessed Sacrament in the monstrance. We need something to look at, to concentrate our thoughts: it is so much more helpful than having just a blank wall or the desert. It's the same with the scent of incense, candles, or the feel of rosary beads in our fingers. We've got to have senses, for we are human beings, creatures of flesh and blood. Instead of trying to deny our senses at prayer we should use them. Let all our senses speak to us of God! When we pray we can begin by listening to the chanted words; every one of them speaks of God, and the sound and the rhythm are there to keep us quiet inside. Then we can fix our eyes on the crucifix, or on the monstrance, and we can know that however much our thoughts wander, whenever we look back at the statue or crucifix or whatever it is, there is something to draw us towards God. We can become aware of the scent of incense, the coloured light from the windows, the feel of the prie-dieu under our knees and the rosary in our hands; and all these things can speak to us of God. This use of the senses is something known to the Church for centuries, and not only the Church but other religions as well. The Tibetan Buddhists have a natural religious instinct to use the things of the senses to make silence of the spirit: their method of prayer consists of repeated phrases and rhythmic chanting and movement. This too our moderns have discovered: many young people now enjoy listening to plainsong. Many recordings have been produced by monasteries and convents, like the nuns at Ryde or the monks at Fontgombauld. They sell quickly because people find to that to have music in the background is a great help to recollection. It is the same with some of the new music that is coming from France such as the Taizé chants. For many people a method of prayer is to put on a tape of something like the Taizé community singing the *Veni Creator Spiritus*, or the monks of Solesmes singing Vespers, as a background to silent contemplation.

That's not something you can do in a convent: if everyone were playing tapes all the time it would be absolutely deafening! But you can have that same sort of musical effect in total silence. By that I mean the long tried and well trusted method of prayer which consists of silently repeating a phrase or a short prayer over and over again. We use words in order to be silent – a paradox, but our faith is full of paradoxes! The most familiar prayer of this sort is the rosary, repeating the words of the 'Hail Mary' over and over again. We don't need to think about the text, although it's quite a long prayer, for we know it so well that it can flow out, one Hail Mary after another, in a great rhythmic heartbeat of prayer. We do not try to attend to the meaning of the words every time; if we were to think through the textual meaning of the Hail Mary one hundred and fifty times a day, it would be absurd. But the meaning is still there, and every word has a meaning. The Eastern tradition is to use the rather shorter prayer to Jesus "Lord Jesus Christ, son of the living God, have mercy on me" in the same way, repeated over and over again. We are familiar with litanies, the glorious rhythm of the Litany of Our Lady, 'pray for us', 'have mercy on us', returning again and again like waves lapping on the seashore. Yet the power of this type of prayer is in the sound, and since we need make no outward noise, we can call it a silent sound which brings peace to our teeming minds. Once we are quiet inside, we can find God. When Elijah went out into the desert he went to the mountain of Horeb, and hid in a cave to hear the word of the Lord. There came a great wind: the Lord was not in the wind. There came a mighty earthquake: the Lord was not in the earthquake. There came a raging fire: the Lord was not in the fire. And then there came the sound of a still small voice, and Elijah heard the Lord in that still small voice. It is in silence and in trust that our hope shall be.

So the most valuable part of a retreat is not the conferences, certainly, but the silence in between the conferences. That is the time to make prayer our own and to listen to that still small voice of God. All I can try to do with words is to remind you of what the Carmelites know much better than I, of how God speaks to us and then hides his face and speaks to us again. If this book is to be of any use, it is better to put it down and be silent than to take it up and read.

PART I

SUN ON THE FOOTHILLS

Chapter One

The Call

Mary, heaven hails you, Mary!
Angels call you, graceful one:
Virgin, make your choice, we hear you;
"Let the Will of God be done!"

The spiritual life has often been compared to a journey, a pilgrimage, a progress from stagnant normality to the glory of God's Kingdom. I shall offer no exception: this book is to be structured around the story of a journey, an actual pilgrimage which I and a group of friends made years ago – the pilgrimage to St James of Compostela. I had vaguely heard of Compostela, but knew little about it, until I happened to light on an article in a magazine describing a pilgrimage. The writer, a priest, described how he and some young parishioners had gone off on this walking pilgrimage: he said how marvellous it was, how they walked in the cool of the morning and slept in the heat of the day and walked on again in the cool of the evening. There were ancient churches and pilgrim hostels on the way. The sun shone, the birds sang and eventually they came to Compostela.

This account led me to think of trying the same thing myself, and so I began to make various inquiries. I didn't inquire anything like enough, as you will hear, but I did as much as I could. I found a book in the library which described the pilgrim route, showing lots of lovely photographs of sun-soaked churches of the south, shady olive trees and enticing taverns. Hilaire Belloc told me about "the fleas that tease in the high Pyrenees, and the wine that tasted of tar." I was warned that "the rain in Spain stays mainly in the plain," so decided to take the mountain route, and I rustled up the appropriate maps: quite good maps for the French part of the route, and what looked like adequate maps for Spain. I worked out just how far it would be, how far I could walk each day, where I would stay. Various contacts and preparations were made, until I was confident that all would go well.

I had heard about the pilgrimage, told other people about it, made a few inquiries and studied my maps; but basically I decided to go on pilgrimage without knowing how it was going to be or when it was going to end. Instead of going somewhere familiar, to a country I had visited before, I would go to a strange country and to a stranger place. I would undertake to be a pilgrim, to set out into the unknown.

Now each of us is at some time called to begin our spiritual pilgrimage through life, but it is remarkable how often our call comes apparently by chance, just as my Compostela pilgrimage was launched by an odd issue of a magazine that was lying around. In our life's journey the call so often comes through chance as remote as that: a magazine, perhaps, scanned in the dentist's waiting room, an old newspaper wrapping your fish and chips, and inside there has been one of those little advertisements for the Catholic Enquiry Centre. You know the sort of thing, a little form to send off for a series of booklets, sent under plain cover. Uncounted thousands of people have begun their pilgrimage through those sort of contacts. Other people come to grace through a chance acquaintance, somebody met on a bus, someone who began a line of thought that eventually leads to realising that God is calling, not someone else but me, to go on pilgrimage with him.

I am talking about two levels of pilgrimage at once. The first is the fundamental vocation to follow Christ in the way of the Christian life, and this seems always to come as if 'by chance'. I suppose like many of us in this country I had the fortune first of all of being born into a Catholic family: but that was just 'by chance'. I could just have easily have been born into a totally

21

pagan family, perhaps from Inner Mongolia or some other area of the world where there was virtually no possibility of ever hearing the Gospel. But the 'chance' has been to be born in a Catholic family. Then there was the 'chance' of being brought up in the right sort of parish, the right sort of school, so that we kept the faith of our baptism. Other people who do not 'chance' to be born into Catholic families are at least born into devout families who follow God as best they can in some other religion. Yet others have no family background of faith at all but again 'by chance' they are sent to school where perhaps they find a Catholic child at the next desk: sometimes Catholic children in non-Catholic schools do a tremendous amount of good! Or they may meet a Catholic in the workplace or even at university. Many of my students became Catholics simply because of people they met. You meet someone, perhaps a bench-mate in the laboratory or a fellow prop-forward on the sports-field or even a fellow propping up the bar; you get to know them and like them and then you discover to your horror that they are Catholics. That sort of 'chance' acquaintance has so often blossomed out into the beginnings of faith and eventually the call to follow Christ in the path of being a Christian, being a Catholic.

Beyond this, within our common Christian vocation, is the special vocation to the religious life or to the priesthood. Here again so often it comes 'by chance'. Many people go happily through life never thinking that they might do anything unusual in the religious line, until perhaps they pass the entrance to a hidden convent somewhere and wonder what lies behind those high walls and locked doors. Or they may meet someone who is about to join a convent, some old friend just off to the seminary. There are so many different ways. I am sure all priests and nuns have their stories about how it was that the call came, how it was 'by chance' that they were chosen to follow Christ on the pilgrimage of prayer. And then of course we realise that chance doesn't come into it at all: I don't really think there is such a thing as chance. We come to realise that what looks to us like sheer coincidence – the fortuitous way the magazine happens to fall open just at the right page – is really carefully planned. "The angels keep their ancient places." I am sure angels spend a lot of time pushing things under people's noses, just making sure they notice them. Angels specialise in making people meet. You see them hovering around in student bars, in workplaces, in bus queues. This 'chance' is directed: it's God's plan, God's call. Once we realise that, we also have to realise (with an appalling sense of humility) that it means our vocation was nothing whatever to do with us. It is entirely a matter of God's grace. We didn't choose him: He chose us. We find ourselves wondering, "Why me? Why us? What have we done to deserve this?" And the answer of course is that we've done absolutely nothing.

That is most obvious when we are chosen from birth. If we were born into a Catholic family, if we have grown up aware of grace in our life, we must admit that we've done absolutely nothing to deserve it, because we were chosen before we were born. We were called; we were baptised; we were offered to God; consecrated to Our Lady; with no choice of our own whatsoever, no chance of claiming any merits or de-merits. It was God who decided, "From all the teeming millions on the earth, I want this one, and this one to be Catholics; and out of those I want this one to be a nun, that one to be a priest." We don't get any say in it. Of course we can say 'No' but we can't say 'Yes'. All we can do is to accept our vocation. Sometimes, sadly, we meet people who would love to have a vocation, but simply haven't got one. There are people who say that they would love to have faith, love to believe in the Catholic Church and all her teachings, but they find that they can't do it. Sometimes you meet people who all their life long have had, as it were, a longing for the faith but can never find it. They have not been chosen, even though their merits seem to be so much greater than ours, and yet we have been chosen. Every nun and every priest knows people who have a longing to be called to the religious life or the priesthood and somehow never are called; they linger perpetually on the fringes of religious life. It is sheer grace that has given us our call: grace also that leaves others without it.

St Paul tells us somewhere that we were chosen before the ages; before the creation began we were destined to be witnesses of God's glory. Paul himself was very conscious of his own call: he had been born to a devout family and brought up in the knowledge of God and the service of the Lord. Then on the road to Damascus he was called, singled out particularly to be the apostle of the Lord: and he was vividly conscious that he had done nothing to deserve this. His birth, his family, his education: these were nothing to boast about. It was just that he happened to be born to a devout family. And again after his conversion he was terribly aware how unworthy he was to be called an apostle. Looking round his congregations in Corinth, Ephesus, Rome and elsewhere he was able to say to them "Remember your call: you were not wise or clever or rich. You had nothing to offer. God chose you apparently at random."

Yet we know that God does nothing at random. What looks like 'chance' has been carefully planned, directed, 'for his own kind purposes'. St Paul is not going to give us any clues what these purposes are for each individual: I don't think he knew himself precisely what was God's plan for him. But God knows exactly what he is doing when he picks on you, or me, and says, "I want you to follow me on the path of prayer." We can easily think of people who would be so much more suitable: we can so often find ourselves advising God, like St Peter who said of St John, "What about him, Lord?" And the Lord says, "Never you mind about him. You follow me." Like Moses we can make all sorts of excuses: he told the Lord clearly that he had called the wrong brother: Aaron was so much better qualified, so much better at public speaking. And the Lord said, "Aaron has indeed his part to play as well, but it is you that I want to talk to Pharoah."

24

As I say, we do have the chance to turn against God altogether. We do have freedom, the freedom to say 'No', to reject our vocation, but we can never actually choose a vocation for ourselves. If we once accept God's will we will find that he does call us, show us our pilgrimage, set us on our way. And all we can do is say, "Yes Lord. You know what you are doing, even if I don't understand it." Pilgrimage is like that. He can give us a few ideas in advance but we never fully understand what we are undertaking. We can begin by asking questions, and enquiring about the Faith. If we're thinking of the religious life we can come to the grille, we can ask "What is it like? What will I have to do? What do I have to be?" We can ask questions and people can try to answer us, they can give us books, pamphlets, and videos. They can give us all sorts of information about what the Christian way, or the monastic way, will mean. And at the end of it we have really very little idea indeed. Sometimes the more we read the promotional literature the less idea we really have of what goes on inside the convent. Some of those outside the Church have studied Catholicism in all its aspects for years but still haven't the remotest idea of what we're really like. We have the opportunity to ask questions; we can ask and we get answers. But in the end we have to make our own decision: "I still don't really know what's going on but, yes, I will go on pilgrimage, I will accept the challenge, I will do whatever needs to be done."

So we are chosen through no merits of our own whatsoever, but this choice brings a terrifying responsibility. That again is something St Paul tells us, that our call is to be responsible for those who are not chosen. God calls us to membership of the Church in this life: if we are faithful now, then in the life to come we can bring with us those who were not so chosen. This certainly seems to be what St Paul is saying in Colossians and Ephesians, in those great hymns that come into the Office so frequently: we are chosen to be the first fruits of God's creation. It doesn't mean that we are destined for heaven and the others are not, as some of the more cruel sects teach. They say that unless you are chosen in this life then you have no hope whatsoever in the next. That's not what the Church tells us, nor what the scriptures teach. We are told that everyone who is acceptable to God and does what is right can get to heaven through the prayers, through the sacrifices, through the offerings of the Church. It is the Church, the first fruit, that is accepted so the rest of humanity is made acceptable. There is no salvation except through the Church, but the Church is the acceptable offering for the salvation of the world.

Within the Church those consecrated in religious life have a responsibility for those 'in the world'. Certainly one can never think of the religious life as a means of getting away from people outside. We have to accept religious life, as we do the priesthood, as something on behalf of those outside. If we withdraw from the world, it is in order to save the world by our prayers. So our choice isn't just a choice for us: it's a choice that carries a responsibility for those who are not chosen. And again the choice is God's choice. We can ask questions about it, but in the end we must accept it with trust, with faith, with love.

Our Lady was chosen in precisely the same way. She was 'chosen before the creation began', marked out before her conception. In God's plan the whole of the Old Testament leads up to the supreme moment when Our Lady accepted her vocation. All former ages were spent in preparation for the time when a sinless Eve could be born to replace the sinful Eve. Thousands of years of history, forty-six books of the Old Testament, tell the story of how God's people struggled back from sin towards righteousness. Gradually they were purified from idolatry and vice; again and again God offered a covenant to his people through the prophets, again and again they fell back into sin, until eventually Our Lady was born. She had no merits of her own whatsoever, she was chosen before she was conceived, chosen to be the culmination of the whole of the Old Testament. That is why she is 'full of grace', since it is pure grace, sheer grace that chose her, that made her conceived immaculate. She was preserved from sin to the age when she was able to accept the message of God for herself. Our Lady was not chosen because of her own efforts or her own merits. The doctrine of the Immaculate Conception, the doctrine of the sinlessness of Mary, emphasises only how great the grace of God is, for the initiative is entirely his. Humankind has very little to offer. Our Lady offered herself 'in her nothingness'. She was nothing, but the Almighty did great things for her. And so she was called, chosen, invited to be the mother of the Saviour.

We don't know the circumstances of that call. Painters love to show Our Lady at her work, spinning or sewing, perhaps not consciously thinking about God at the time, although her life was so drenched with God that she could never be far away. Other painters show her praying at the moment of the call. But it was not something that she would anticipate; it seemed almost by chance that the angel happened to be passing that day. And yet we know that it was no chance: it was the moment the whole of creation had been waiting for from the very beginning.

Our Lady is not ashamed to ask questions. She wants to know what this is going to involve, how is this going to be. And the angel tells her just a little about it: "Power from the most high shall come upon you. You shall call his name Jesus." And I think Our Lady realises then that she's not going to understand all that is involved. The angel couldn't possibly tell her everything that's going to ensue. She has no idea what will happen if she says yes. But St Bernard, in one of his sermons, has this lovely picture of all the angels of heaven leaning over in expectation to see whether she is going to say yes. Because she still has the freedom: like the first Eve she has the freedom to say no. Because the first Eve too was conceived immaculate and brought up sinless, but when she was given the choice she said no. So the angels who watched the fall of man were once again watching and listening. There was, as it were, a moment of suspense in heaven. And she, she doesn't know what she is taking on. She cannot see the path of the pilgrimage leading on to Egypt, to Nazareth, to Jerusalem and out to Calvary, nor how it would lead on again to Ephesus, to Walsingham and to Lourdes.

Our Lady said, "Yes. Be it done unto me according to thy word." That's all any of us can say. God calls us to our pilgrimage in life, calls us into the religious life. He goes on calling us every day to keep following the way. All we can ever say at the end of the day, when we've asked all our questions and made all our plans, thought all our thoughts, and considered all our objections, all we can ever say at the end is, "Be it done unto me according to thy word."

Chapter Two

Gathering a Company

In the heart of Mary's cousin
See the unborn child rejoice:
At the visit of the Virgin,
At the song of her pure voice.

Once I had decided I would go on pilgrimage the first stage was for 'I' to become 'we'. It did not seem sensible to set off on anything like that on my own, so I had to find other people foolish enough to go with me. Now this was when I was working as a Chaplain in the central area of London University, so I cast the net around the Chaplaincy and enticed some and persuaded others. A few were willing to come and the rest ran as soon as they saw me approach, but between us, eventually, a group assembled.

Some of these people I already knew quite well, others I had only met occasionally, while one joined us at her brother's instigation without knowing any of us before. They came from many different places and different backgrounds, and not all of them were students. Some of them knew the languages, some of them knew how to pray, and some of them knew practical things like how to cook and where to set up camp; when to pack up again, and how to find our way in the jungles and marshes of Southern France and Northern Spain. On the whole the boys were the more devout, though there was one very efficient character who carried all sorts of useful things in a vast rucksack which he called 'Henry'. He could make tea under any circumstances, and played the penny whistle. On the whole the girls were more practical, though less pious: they could, among other things, speak Spanish. It was a very mixed group but as a set of people we were able to help each other. To begin with we met to plan, to advise each other on what to take and what to leave behind. When we actually started on our pilgrimage we were there to encourage each other, to keep each other going, even to sing to each other when things got bad. One was an incorrigible singer, while the penny whistle kept us going for hour after hour as we walked along following various tunes picked up in various places. The pilgrimage became not a solitary venture but a communal one: it was as a group that we set off for Compostela.

In the same way, our pilgrimage through life must be communal, we do it as a group, we do it together. We are never on our own. It may seem strange, but you do get people occasionally who say "I want to be a Christian but I don't see any need for the Church. I don't want to have anybody else around me. I want to be an anonymous Christian." There have indeed been odd people who have gone through their Christian life or attempted to go through a Christian life purely on their own. They claim to be converts to Christianity but not to any Church; they refuse to have anything to do with any Christian community. These are the sort who mutter about "not having to go to Church to be a Christian," or even "worshipping under the great blue dome of heaven." But that is not what Our Lord offers us: he offers us a community. From the very beginning there were twelve apostles, then seventy-two disciples, then five hundred of them at once, three thousand converts in one day.... At the last count there were well over a billion of us.

Our Lord offers us not a solitary path but a common one, and that's why our call to faith is always a call into the Church. We are not alone in our Christian journey. We don't have to find our own way in the dark, or give ourselves the necessary support to keep going. We are together in the Church. If we're confused about what to do or where to go, what to believe or how to behave, we are helped by being part of a body, the Body of Christ, which is the Church.

Our Christian life begins surrounded by other people: Godparents who present us at the font, the priest or deacon, our own parents, family and friends. We also call on our siblings the saints, in a litany to remind us that we are all one family. We call God 'Our Father', we welcome Our Lady as mother, and acknowledge so many millions of brothers and sisters. We enter the Church in a gathering, and the same is true if we enter religious life. You can't begin by being a solitary: you begin religious life in a community, in a noviciate with other people. Perhaps the most difficult as well as the most sustaining part of religious life is coping with the others: St Philip Neri used to say that "community life is the greatest of mortifications," but we do need to be together.

Nobody can be a monk on his own; nobody can be a nun on her own, though some have tried. St Benedict thought he could do it: he ran away from university in Rome and went off into the hills to try and be a monk all on his own, and after a fairly short experiment realised that it wouldn't do. It couldn't be done alone, inexperienced, unformed. In the wisdom of maturity he formed communities and eventually wrote his Rule in which he outlines a way of life for monks who live in common, or 'coenobites'. True, he refers to the solitaries with respect, the 'strong race of anchorites', but emphasises that nobody should be allowed to be an anchorite or hermit who has not been proved and tried by many years in the community. The same point has been discovered by a great many amateur hermits. You can't be a religious on your own unless you know how to be a religious in community. That's why the only successful hermits in history have been people who were well able to live in community, had found their way and walked on their path together. To live on one's own is a very rare vocation and I am sure that the vocation to be a hermit can only be genuine if it is accepted for the sake of other people. The hermit withdraws from people only because he loves people, other members of the community and the Church at large. Most of us do not love other people enough, and so we have to be coenobites all our life. (The thing to avoid above all is being a drifter, like the dreadful false monks St Benedict calls 'sarabites' or 'gyrovagues', of whom it is better to keep silence.)

Christian life as we know it is based on companionship and friendship. A community based on friendship is one that flourishes, one that continues. That is something which comes across very obviously in the letters and the life of St Teresa. Her communities, with all their problems, were to be communities of friends. That's why she wanted to keep them small, having for many years put up with life in a community that was much too big. The community should be small so that everyone can know and love everyone else. All the great monastic writers say the same: the community of brothers, or of sisters, the Christian family, must be a community of love, because we are walking on our pilgrimage together.

It is true that there have been ascetics in the Church who have tried to deny that element of community, but theirs is not the authentic tradition. There were perhaps writers in the past who implied that there should be no human affection, no love in a religious community, that you should just exist side by side, not together. But if you read the real saints it's very clear that their lives are full of love, alive with friendship, which is why the best monasteries and convents radiate a family feeling. It's one of the nicest things about visiting such a convent or a monastery, to find this atmosphere of love. I remember years ago staying in a large Benedictine abbey, where on the way out from Compline, before climbing the stairs to the dormitory, each one stopped to get the abbot's fatherly blessing. It was like watching a large family trooping up to bed, with their father at the bottom of the stairs wishing them good night. There were about thirty-five monks, but still there was a strong feeling that they were all one family. This seemed like the sort of monastery where St Benedict would have felt at home.

Many of the great spiritual writers speak of the companionship we need in human life, because, as the scriptures say right at the beginning, God said "It is not good for man to be alone." We are created in the image and likeness of God, and God is not alone: God is a Trinity. If we're going to live in the image of the Trinity, our life has to be one of love in respect of other people. God calls us to come together in this Christian vocation, to support each other, to give each other the encouragement and friendship we need – as well as sometimes to provide for each other the necessary challenges, in overcoming which we become saints. If a person is particularly difficult, you can think of that person as the one with the vocation to help you to be a saint. That is our job in life: to help each other to be saints. We are not meant to be alone. We are not meant to be isolated. We are meant to love each other as Christ has loved us. Our Lord repeats this in the Gospel again and again, in different ways, in actions, parables and straight teaching. St John picked this up from the Lord, and to the end of his life preached over and over again, "Little children, love one another."

Now obviously there is a wrong sort of love as well as the right sort of love and all the spiritual writers warn us against the exclusive love, what we call the 'particular' friendship, when two or three people group together and exclude everybody else. There's nothing more destructive of a Christian family than that. If two sisters are always together and will not speak to anybody else or are conspiring together against the family, then it destroys their own spiritual life as well as everybody else's. That is why exclusive friendship is not in fact love at all, indeed St Aelred insists that it is so different that a different word should be found for it. Here we are talking about genuine friendship. The love of the brethren that Our Lord commands for us is a love that is always going outwards, always wider and always open. So in a religious community love within the community is something which should be building up the entire community, always open to new members. I suppose it is possible danger that a community could become so friendly towards each other that they have no room for novices. Well, Christian love, Christian friendship, is always willing to expand, willing to move out to new people.

St Aelred it was who wrote most clearly and most beautifully about the duties and the difficulties and the joy in Christian friendship. He was actually living in a very large community indeed, the great abbey of Rievaulx. I gather there were well over a hundred monks, and many more lay-brothers: far too big a household, we would think, to have any feeling of family. But it is clear from the writings of St Aelred that he was able to form that into a loving community of people who helped each other on their way.

I suppose the simple test of Christian love and Christian friendship is, does this association, do these people, help me to get closer to Christ? Friendship that is taking us away from Christ is not a friendship at all, it's an enmity. A friendship that is leading us towards Christ is a reflection of the friendship, the love within the Trinity. That is the true foundation of every religious order, to be 'founded on love, rooted in love'. You cannot have a religious order that is purely practical, that has no element of Christian love in it. This is so clearly stated in the writings of the great monastic saints. St Teresa is always talking about the real affection she has for some of her nuns. She is not ashamed to admit that there are some nuns that she finds easier to get on with than others. There is nothing incompatible with Christian fellowship in having special friends even within the community. One of St Teresa's letters to a prospective novice says something like, "I do hope you'll come and join this particular community that I'm in at the moment, because I want to get to know you. I want to have you near me." There is always room for a special friendship as long it's not exclusive. It is clear from the writings of St Teresa that she had great friendships, great affections for the different nuns and the friars of her order and yet her love, her friendship was always building, growing outwards, full of the light and the love of God. St Aelred was the same: he speaks openly about his special friends within the monastery, and yet in his dialogues you can see how more and more people come in and there's never any element of exclusion. They are going together on pilgrimage and the group that goes on pilgrimage is getting larger and larger.

As I say, that is something which members of religious orders are used to, but can be a particular difficulty for diocesan priests. They alone in the Church seem to have to walk alone, and it is one of the reasons why so often diocesan priests have difficulties in their vocations. Every generation sees a need to reform the lonely clergy, because it is so very difficult to have true friends in the secular priesthood. The problem is that every saint who attempts to reform the way of life of ordinary clergy seems to found a religious order instead, as it were by mistake. There are lots of organisations and fraternities, but still too many isolated friendless priests. That is something to commend to the prayers of the nuns: that we can overcome the fear or diffidence which prevents secular priests from finding real friends, whether among parishioners or fellow priests, for it is only if we know how to love that we can lead both people and religious in the common pilgrimage with Christ.

The lay Christian too may find herself isolated, especially the new convert. It can be very daunting joining an established parish, where everyone gives the impression of knowing each other, even more daunting to join one where no one seems to know anyone else, but all scuttle away as soon as Mass is ended. It takes courage and perseverance to enter into parish life, to find support and association among fellow-Catholics, but it is necessary to make this effort, to persevere in trying to penetrate the circles of parish organisations and groups. Because no one is called to be a lonely Christian.

Our model for the Christian life is, as always, Our Lady. As soon as she heard the angel's message she went as quickly as she could to the hill country of Judea to visit Elizabeth. She went to find friendship and to give friendship, to help Elizabeth in what might be a rather difficult time, being well past the age of childbirth. St Luke tells us that Our Lady stayed till St John the Baptist was born. She was there to help in very practical ways, to take over the running of the house, to cook Zachariah's meals for him. She was there in love and fellowship and companionship. And at the same time surely Our Lady found help and love and support from Elizabeth. It was not a one-sided relationship, for Elizabeth, the older woman with the dignity and maturity of age, was able to help Our Lady, just as Our Lady helped Elizabeth. And although the Gospels tell us no more about that friendship, yet it's a sound Christian instinct to imagine that Our Lady and Elizabeth remained close friends, and that John the Baptist and Our Lord grew up together. There are many famous paintings which show the two children playing, the two mothers talking to each other, perhaps getting on with their spinning the while. There was friendship and fellowship within the extended Holy Family, as there needs to be in every human soul. Our Lady became the friend and helper of so many people, beginning with Elizabeth. We see her at the marriage of Cana in her concern for the bride and groom; there she is at the foot of the cross, taken into the family of St John; there at last in the Acts of the Apostles as the Mother of the Church.

The first description ever given of the Church is, "the apostles gathered round Mary the mother of Jesus," so she is never seen alone. By being with her we need never be alone either. Our journey, our pilgrimage, needs companions, and they are never difficult to find if we are open and allow the Lord to choose them for us. If we make our own choices then often we'll choose the wrong ones. If we allow Our Lord and Our Lady to choose our companions, they will often be people we would never have dreamt of, but we will find ourselves on the way, supported by people with different talents, different abilities, different characters. Some will support us directly and some will support us indirectly, but we will be on our way together. And so we can set off with some confidence on our pilgrimage to Compostela.

Chapter Three

The Birth of Joy

Shepherds, angels, kings and oxen
Bend to see their tiny Lord;
Mary lays her love before us,
Wrapt in bands, the living Word.

Once we had made a start, we found it was very pleasant going
on pilgrimage. The sun shone but was not too hot, we found
friendly people on the way, and the food and wine were excellent.
We began in Paris, by visiting the church of St Jacques du Haut-
Pas, which is where the pilgrimages traditionally started in the
Middle Ages. The curé gave us a good welcome, we celebrated
Mass with him, and were given a great send-off by the good
parishioners. So we wandered on our way down through France.
Sometimes we stayed in friendly convents, sometimes we camped
out in nice dry woods. The route lay along pleasant little country
lanes meandering between the farms. At other times we were
on footpaths, miles from any habitation. We lay on grassy banks
by cool streams for lunch, watching great birds of prey hovering
overhead, as we approached the Pyrenees. In the small towns and
villages we found very cheap restaurants where we ate extremely
well for very little.

In every village were quaint little churches, especially in the
Basque country, where every church had a pelota court attached
to it. (Pelota is an obscure Basque ritual which seems to occupy
the place of cricket in their national spirituality.) The Basque
people, in their little black berets, were very friendly, and spoke
French to us out of politeness. So all in all we found that going
on pilgrimage was really very pleasant indeed. It fulfilled our

expectations of wandering gently in the cool of the morning and the cool of the evening, while in the heat of the day we could sit under a tree by the side of a river and have our lunch, watching the birds and little white fluffy clouds moving across the sky.

When we start our pilgrimage it's always like that, isn't it? The path of faith, the path of prayer, always seems to begin so very pleasantly. The fervour of the new convert or the youngest novice is proverbial. It is always a great joy to begin the Christian path and we do find it very pleasant as soon as we've made our acceptance and said, "Be it done unto me according to thy word." There don't seem to be any problems in following God's will: in fact we wonder why it is that some of the older members of the community, some of the more established Christians, seem to have lost that fervour. We may even be rather scornful of them, because we know that we have received the joy of God's grace, and feel that they should be just as joyful.

New converts find it a great joy to come to church; in fact it's difficult to get them out when it's time to lock up. New novices act in the same way: for them it is always a great joy to praise the Lord. There is a real joy in everything, particularly any form of prayer, because prayer is made easy for us. The Mass becomes the source of our joy and the source of our pleasure and we find that it doesn't matter to us whether it is in Latin or English, good music or bad, new music or old. We're not really bothered about the externals of the liturgy because the Mass itself, the joy of the great sacrifice, speaks to us. We know that Christ is born in our hearts in Holy Communion; for the convert, the one newly started on the Way of the Cross, there is a real feeling of pleasure in receiving Our Lord in the Blessed Sacrament. We wonder why following Jesus is ever called the Way of the Cross, since for us it seems to be a way of gentleness and kindness, a way lined with flowers, a very peaceful way in which Our Lord leads us by the hand.

If Mass is a joy, so too is the Divine Office, as we gladly join our fellow parishioners, our brothers or sisters, singing the praises of the Lord. We feel that the Office could go on for ever. No matter how long the Psalms are, the great rhythm of the music carries us on. We feel an exultation inside us as the Lord allows the Holy Spirit to speak in our hearts, to give us that praise of the Father. Every time we recite the Psalms we find another jewel in the text, another phrase, another few words that really mean something. They can stay with us all day: we go through our daily life, even doing the most ordinary things of life, almost skipping for joy as we remember a phrase that we picked up in the Psalms, some word that's fallen from the scriptures, some word of the Mass.

Even private prayer, even mental prayer seems to be so very easy. When we begin to pray it is no effort just to put ourselves in the presence of the Lord and to be quiet before him. Concentration is never a difficulty: we can sit or kneel there gazing spellbound at the Blessed Sacrament. Prayer comes naturally to us now: there is no need to think of words. The last thing we want to do is to look and see how the time is passing. It's a disappointment when the bell strikes and we have to go and do something else. Then it's so easy to remember our friends at prayer, to place them before the Lord, so easy to remember all those who've asked our prayers, gently to mention them, to dwell on them lovingly in the presence of the Lord. Somehow prayer, the Mass, liturgy, the Office, everything seems delightful. The danger is lest we become very critical indeed of those crabbed old members of the community who don't seem to enjoy it so much; them we find impossible to understand.

In the same way the duties of the Christian life seem so very simple. It's a real joy to do good, to perform little acts of charity. You will remember how St Teresa describes her own noviciate: it was a joy to her to do some little thing for an elderly sister and she found it difficult to get to sleep at night if she couldn't remember having done some good work for someone. What a relief if, just as she was preparing for bed, she heard one of the older sisters stumbling up the steps: Teresa was able to rush out and help her up to her room. There is a real joy in serving other people; and so for the Christian in the world, who is just beginning the life of grace, there is true joy in doing practical works of mercy. It is the new converts who are eager to join the Society of St Vincent de Paul or the Legion of Mary, who are absolutely delighted when they get a chance to go out into the council estate or to the tower blocks to find a family in need. They really feel a pleasure. It is characteristic that they find the pleasure in anticipation, enjoying the prospect of going to Mass, beginning to pray, visiting the poor, even attending parish meetings. This pleasure of anticipation is followed by pleasure while we are actually working or praying, and again afterwards we feel happy to have done God's will. This glorious period of fervour is a very genuine and very real gift from the Lord. Because what Our Lord is doing for the new convert is allowing Christ to be born in their soul, so that they are filled with the reality of Christian life.

Of course it is our own imagination that tells us, "I am now a perfect Christian, a perfect novice, a perfect deacon or whatever. There is nothing more to live for." That is always the danger with the new convert. We think we've won: there is no further to go. "Here I am. Christ has been born in my heart. I am filled with grace." And it is genuine grace: we recognise it as such. There need not be an element of pride. We can accept and be grateful for this gift of prayer, this gift of the love of God, this gift of love for others, the fact that it's so easy to cope with the difficult ones, that we are able to smile benignly on the most repulsive people. All these graces we humbly recognise to be gifts from God and there is no reason not to revel in this great welling of joy which is the first fruits of grace in our hearts.

The danger is of course to think that this is as far as it goes. It does indeed happen that new converts fall into the trap, the terrible trap, of spiritual pride. They fondly imagine that there is nothing more to live for, they are certainly going to heaven, everything is sorted out in life; and they are so terribly liable to despise the rest of humanity, especially those who call themselves Christians, but really don't seem to have that Christian joy. Particularly among young people, among students, you find that when God's grace is first born in their hearts they can be very critical indeed of old established Christians, even going to the extreme of wondering whether we are really Christians at all if we don't display that visible tangible joy all the time. That is obviously a peril, and one to be always on the watch for, since spiritual pride can arise in various disguises and various pious concealments. Yet there is no need to fall into this trap, and with common decency and humility, a fervent new convert or new novice can unashamedly enjoy and really make the most of that birth of Christ in their souls.

So it was with Our Lady. She travelled from Nazareth to Bethlehem, knowing that she had the friendship, the support and the love of Elizabeth and her family, and of Saint Joseph (to say nothing of Saints Joachim and Anne, who seem to have been left behind in Nazareth). She comes to Bethlehem and Christ is born! And in that moment of the birth of Our Lord, Our Lady must have felt that all was accomplished. Here is Christ born; the whole of the Old Testament has come to its fulfilment, since God and man have been made one. Those first few days were glorious, when Our Lady saw the hope of all the ages placed in her bosom; she saw the joy of the angels, the glory of all the saints, made flesh in her stable, in her swaddling clothes; she felt the awe with which the shepherds knelt, the joyful awe. They came in love, they came in excitement. And then the strange pacing of the magi, those proud men brought from afar, brought humble before a child in a stable. The glory of the angels ... surely if the shepherds saw the angels, Our Lady cannot have failed to hear their song!

Mary's heart was filled with the glory of the birth of Christ: how could she imagine that there was more to come? Those few days in Bethlehem: how could she think there was anything more?

The path of being the Mother of God surely seemed to be one of unadulterated joy. Maybe she did look ahead, or maybe she saw nothing of what was coming. But for those few days at any rate she could hardly have thought of the future. All her thoughts must have been filled with the joy of knowing that Christ has been born.

Christ was truly born; it was no illusion. This joy at the beginning of our Christian life is perfectly genuine. It is a real grace, a real joy and a real birth of Christ in our souls. But of course, as Our Lady was all too soon to see, there still can be a sword of sorrow, still a long way to go. The path to glory leads ever past the cross. That is why so often in our paintings of the crib you see the infant Jesus stretching out his arms in the form of the cross as if to show us that, yes, this joy, this glory is perfectly real, but there is sorrow to come.

Chapter Four

Fitting in

In the solemn Temple precinct
See the ancient ritual start:
Hear the old man's words of foresight;
Mary ponders in her heart.

Once we were on our way it did not take us long to realise that when you're visiting a strange country, however near, you have to conform to their way of doing things (well, we had guessed it before, actually). Their laws, their customs, are different from ours, and the traveller must at least try to fit in. For walkers the first obvious difference is that the French will insist on driving on the wrong side of the road, so that to face the traffic we have to walk on what for us would be the wrong side of the road too. It was surprisingly difficult to remember that.

Among other things we had to fit in with were the curious hours at which their shops open. We had to remember to buy our provisions and anything else we needed on the way at the right moment. Even when the shop was open, they had their own ways of running things: for instance it appeared to be necessary to produce an empty wine bottle to hand in before they would let us have a full one. We had to remember that there were certain times during the day when you can get a meal and certain times when you can't. In small villages in France we found it easy to get lunch, but supper seemed to be quite unheard of. We settled eventually into a routine of a picnic breakfast and supper, and lunch in a little café. In Spain, on the other hand, they did serve meals in the evening, but everything in Spain happened so much later that lunch was not served before two in the afternoon and dinner not much before ten. All the way along we had to adjust to the people we walked among, to speak their language, do things their way, fit into their customs. We were guests in a foreign country, trying as far as possible to accommodate ourselves to their way of life.

Now if we are on a pilgrimage of grace, a pilgrimage towards the heavenly city of Jerusalem, we are also in a sense pilgrims in a foreign land. This present world is not our real homeland, as St Paul tells us; our homeland is in heaven, but to begin with we do not feel at home there. We have to adjust to the customs, fit into the way of life, of our eternal homeland. Their customs are very different to ours. We've been used to living according to the laws and customs of this world, and there is an enormous amount of change to be made, an enormous amount of adjustment to our daily habits, to our whole way of life, if we're going to walk on the pilgrimage with Christ.

Simply becoming a Christian, having been born a pagan, makes an enormous difference. Taking on the religious life brings a great difference again. There are new rules to be kept, new laws to observe, new standards to aim at. An outsider looking at us on pilgrimage, would wonder how on earth we can remember all these laws. How can we possibly keep track of all the things we have to do and all the things we have to avoid? To the outsider it must seem as if the Christian life is spent in continual reference to the rulebook. Can we never do anything without flipping through the Old Testament, counting up the ten commandments, and seeing which of them we're breaking at the moment?

But of course it isn't really like that at all. If Christ has been born in us, if we have started on our pilgrimage, if we have received the grace and the joy, and the life of Christ living in us, all these rules and regulations somehow become so much simpler. That again is something very characteristic of the first fervour of conversion, the first fervour of religious life. To keep the moral law of God, or the rules of the order, seems to be so very, very easy. We wonder again why older members find them so difficult. To begin with it is no longer a problem to remember what the rules are: we know instinctively what we ought to do. The reason for that is that our conscience becomes more and more reliable as we give ourselves to Christ, as we allow the new life, the Holy Spirit to dwell in us. It's the Holy Spirit speaking inside us that is our conscience, and the more we allow the Spirit to work, the clearer he can speak.

The new Christian, therefore, no longer has to search and puzzle, to plough through the Old Testament to look up the ten commandments, and the Catechism to find out whether something is a sin or not; you know instinctively that it is. We have an ever sharper instinct for what is right. Jesus himself said in the Gospel, "Why not judge for yourselves what is right?" And once we've begun on our pilgrimage we are able to judge for ourselves. We do find that God's laws make sense; they are not arbitrary obstacles put in our way to make Christian life more difficult. No, God's laws are there to make life easier and we discover, if we are beginning to be in love with Christ, that doing his will becomes much more desirable. In the same way in the first fervour of religious life, doing the work, saying the Office, living according to the rule, all becomes so very enjoyable. We cannot understand how anyone could want to be a religious without attempting to keep every detail of the rule.

Of course there is a big difference between acknowledging the law and being able to keep it. I think the ability to keep God's law is something that comes in stages, but it does begin in the first fervour of Christian life as we feel the joy of prayer, the joy of the Mass, the joy of the sacraments. You find that it becomes easier and easier to keep the moral law, to keep the rule of the order. People commonly follow a pattern of development as they strive to come closer to Christ. To begin with, many have been struggling for years against a habit of sin; perhaps at first they don't really believe it's a sin, not in their heart of hearts, but they confess it because the Catechism says they should. Then they come to the stage of realising that it is indeed the will of God that they should overcome this habit: it really is something dragging them away from Christ. And then, as they grow in the life of prayer, suddenly, unexpectedly, it becomes possible. I have met so many people who tell me that for years they never believed they could possibly overcome their particular besetting sin. They were quite resigned that this was going to be with them forever, and they almost automatically, whenever they went to confession, used the same words, as if they had despaired of the work of grace. And then at last God speaks, and the problem disappears, sometimes so suddenly and completely that they can never quite believe it had ever happened.

Once you start on pilgrimage, once you start setting aside time every day for prayer, you will find prayer easy and joyful. If you have established a habit of good works, they too become something you are eager to do: now it is a real pleasure to give to the poor. Again in the first fervour of conversion, so many people find fasting delightful. With a regular routine of self-denial suddenly the old habits of sin somehow disappear. People say to me sometimes, "But it was so easy, Father. Why couldn't I do it before?" And the answer of course is you didn't do it. It was the grace of God working in you. God does make it possible for us to keep his laws. He does make it possible for us to keep the rules of our order, or even to be obedient to a superior, for the clergy to give our bishop the obedience and respect we promised him at our ordination, and which we commonly find so difficult.

Christian sanctity is actually possible. This joy of Christ is born in our lives because he comes to lead us gently on our pilgrimage. Without him we really would wander astray. Without his guidance it would be so easy to lose our path, to turn aside into marshes and desert places or to give up altogether. With him there to guide us, pointing out the way, it becomes a well marked pilgrimage-route. At every step of the way there is a signpost, but we find we don't even need to look at them because our path is obvious, as we instinctively follow our conscience. We find it's possible to see what is good and to do it, to know what is bad and avoid it. That is why in the first fervour of conversion so many people speak of old habits of sin overcome, old problems long forgotten.

As I said, the danger is that people become very intolerant of those who don't seem to have overcome their problems yet. It can be very difficult for the newly fervent, the newly converted, to understand why some of the older members seem to have so much difficulty in keeping the rules, so much more trouble with the elementary commandments. It can be very hard to be tolerant of them, and the fervour of the new convert often has to be moderated with a degree of understanding and compassion. Yet again that is sickeningly easy for some of them: once you point out that we are commanded to forgive others as we hope to be forgiven, you find the new convert eagerly going around forgiving everyone in sight. The joy of being able to follow God's law and the tremendous sense of liberation and peace which it brings is a gift which Christ surely does give to us. It's a perfectly genuine gift and, as in the case of the gift of joy, the temptation is to think, with innocent complacency, "There is nothing more to live for in Christian life. I've reached perfection, I will never sin again. I must be already at the goal of my pilgrimage."

Perhaps that is why Our Lord always reminds us, very gently, that there are still problems to come. It may well be that having overcome one besetting sin you suddenly discover there was something else much worse which we never even noticed – although our friends may have been quite aware of it all the time! It may be that some wise director, or some word in the scripture, points out the next stage, gives us a friendly warning. But we should savour this moment of joy, this time of grace, for it is genuine, a real gift from God. It is time that we must use well to prepare for the difficulties which are still to come.

So it was with Our Lady. She took Jesus to the temple to be

presented according to the Law of Moses, that every firstborn should be offered to God and a sacrifice should be given in celebration of this gift of a child. And also that the mother should be purified so that after the great holiness of childbirth she could be able to return to ordinary everyday life. So they fulfilled the commandments – not just the commandments of the law but even the little rules made up by the scribes and Pharisees. We are reminded many times in the gospels that there is a difference between the Law which God revealed to Moses and the 'traditions of the elders' which were wrapped around the law like a hedge in order to protect it. Our Lady and St Joseph didn't quibble and they didn't distinguish, they observed the law and they respected the tradition of the elders, and they carried out precisely and meticulously what was expected of them. They brought two young pigeons and they said the necessary prayers, they made the necessary offering in the temple.

They offered the sacrifice for the redemption of the one who is himself the Redeemer, for the purification of her who was the most pure. Did St Joseph and Our Lady fully grasp, the true significance of who this Child was? Surely they could not have understood it all so soon: but at least they must have known that to redeem the Redeemer was a work that was unnecessary. They must have known that there was no need for purification, there was no need for the presentation. And yet they did it to fit in with the law of God's people, to be obedient in all things to the law.

The Pharisees and scribes, reading through the Old Testament, found six hundred and thirteen separate commandments, of which two hundred and forty eight were positive requirements, and three hundred and sixty five were prohibitions: all had to be obeyed. These formed the Torah, and around them are the innumerable precepts of the Mishnah and the Talmud, a very complicated and very difficult system of law to observe. Has there ever been a Jewish family who managed to keep it all, except the Holy Family? Surely in Our Lady's kitchen everything was prepared precisely according to the Jewish law: I am confident she never boiled milk in a meat saucepan. So it was in their house and in their dress: when Our Lady made a seamless garment for Our Lord it must have had tassels in precisely the right places, of just the right length, as laid down in the traditions of the elders. Everything was done to fit in with the laws of God's people even though Our Lady was well aware that those traditions were passing away, even though she knew that her Son was the one who made that law. He it was for the sake of whom all those laws had been made; the whole ritual of purification in the temple was only instituted for the sake of the one who was to come to the temple and purify it, for the sake of Jesus himself. But they observed the law, they submitted to it, giving a model of obedience and humility.

And yet we still occasionally meet people who imagine themselves above the law. They consider that they have reached a higher state of perfection than the mere mortals around them. Our Lady really was superior to the law, she really had reached a higher state of perfection, but she never for a moment thought that she could disobey the law. She remained faithful and lived according to it. So too did Our Lord: he observed the Jewish law right through his life. Yet he himself said this observance was a burden too heavy to be borne, that no one could obey it except through grace, and so it was only through grace that Our Lady was able to obey the whole of the law. That grace gave her great joy. There is no reason to assume that she found it in the slightest bit difficult or inconvenient to obey the law. She obeyed the law because it was the law of God, the law of God's people, and God was the great lover of her soul. She found a great joy in observing the law of Presentation, in coming to the temple and carrying out the ritual – and at the very moment of her joy Simeon appears at her side and says, "A sword of sorrow shall pierce your own soul too." It is with that warning that Our Lady remembers, or perhaps she realises for the first time, that there is a great deal more to be done. This joy is a sound and firm foundation for her life, but there is sorrow to come. So she listens to Simeon; she remembers his warning; she ponders all these things in her heart.

Chapter Five

Loss and Gain

Lost in Zion's holy city
Jesus wanders all alone:
Mary, Joseph, search and find Him
Safe within His Father's home.

In Spain, it appears, the rain stays exclusively on the mountains: it began as we reached the Pyrenees. They were not very high at the point where we crossed them, but still quite a barrier. Not really high enough to look pretty, either: there were neither snow-capped peaks nor glaciers, but just a rather bleak-looking range of very steep hills – and came the rain.

The route led us up the haunted pass of Roncevaux. We had to camp half way up, as thunder rumbled vaguely around in the distance, and there was a general uncertainty in the air as to whether it was going to start raining seriously or not. Then in the middle of the night we were woken by the sound of galloping horses. We saw nothing but we heard them galloping, sounding as if they were coming right through the camp. Were we about to be trampled on – what was the meaning of these heavy cavalry horses pounding up the pass, the sound of a horn blowing in the distance?

The next day was grey and drizzly, the sort of misty day when you can't see more than a few yards in front of you. The way was well marked but tedious. Water began to trickle down the path. Then eventually it trickled into our boots, into our rucksacks. Plodding up the hills we were beginning to wonder if the pilgrimage was such a good idea after all. At the top we found the Spanish border, which only meant that the path stopped being so well marked, and there was a line of wire to stop Spanish sheep straying into France or the other way round. There was no sign of anybody trying to stop us, check our passports or ask how many sheep we were hoping to smuggle across (Spain was still independent in those days). We skipped over the little wire and wandered on, across a rather bleak, windswept, rain-soaked, misty summit, until eventually we came to a ridge – and there the sun broke through! We found we were right on the crest of the pass, and just below us on the Spanish side the sunlight glistened on the tin roof of the great abbey of Roncesvalles.

So we came merrily down the path to the abbey, where we were greeted warmly by the community, few though they were. The buildings are vast: there must be room for eighty monks, well, Canons Regular to be precise, but then there were only three. They made us very welcome and offered us a choice of rooms to sleep in, plenty of hot water, food, and shelter; and we celebrated Mass with them. It appeared that being on pilgrimage wasn't really so bad after all. In the evening we talked to some students coming the other way from Spain. I remember they asked us to explain why on earth we were doing this, and one of us said, "It's always worth while doing something a little bit difficult for God." And we nodded together at that: wasn't it marvellous, we had done something difficult for God and we've come over this wet, wind-swept hill and here we are! Isn't pilgrimage such a good thing to be doing!

The rains come in every Christian life, don't they! Unexpectedly, just when we think everything is going so well, in the new fervour of our conversion, suddenly, unaccountably, everything seems to go wrong. And we find that the joy has disappeared from our Christian life. It can be very puzzling if we've become accustomed to our time of fervour, however long or short it has been. For some people it is all of five hours, while others keep it up for a year or so, but sooner or later the period of a convert's fervour or a novice's joy expires. And we are left wondering, "What have we done wrong? Why has the Lord done this to us? Why has he suddenly hidden himself?"

We can get quite frustrated as we find that the things of God no longer please us. The Mass, once such a joy, begins to become extremely irritating. This is when we notice the variations in the Liturgy. We feel particularly vexed that it's no longer the way we were used to. Things are being changed: a new priest turns up and decides to do things his way. And as we get more and more irritated, we spend more and more of the Mass saying, "If only he would do it that way instead of this way. If only we were still allowed to do the other thing. If only we could change this into that." The Mass becomes one long series of distractions. If we are nuns we are tempted to envy those in the world outside, who at least have the freedom to choose where to go for Mass. But if we already are in the world outside, our delusion is to wander from church to church, trying to find a priest who will do the Mass precisely the way we want; and strangely, we never seem to find him! As for us priests, we spend our time longing to have the courage to change something, or wracked with anger at parishioners or bishops who frustrate our efforts to perform the perfect liturgy.

It goes on, till in the end attending Mass is something no longer to look forward to but something to dread. That sinking feeling on a Sunday morning: "Oh dear! I've got to go to Mass!" The lovely feeling on a weekday morning: "There's no obligation to go to Mass today." Then we feel, "There's no need to get there too early: I'll just arrive in time for the Gospel. Perhaps I'll arrive after the collection." The feeling of "Let's put it off as long as possible. I can't cope with Mass in the morning. I'll go in the evening." And then the Mass itself is just one series of irritations after another.

It's the same with prayer, the same with the Office. We try to say the Office, but suddenly we realise quite how long and boring some of the Psalms are. Or we discover that some of the Psalms have been bowdlerised, bits have been missed out which might shock our modern susceptibilities, and we start getting annoyed at that. Then we decide that really the Antiphons are too irritating for words and some of them really don't make sense at all. And as for the Intercessions, they're impossible! So the Office also becomes something to dread. Then if there's an extra bit added on, or if it's going more slowly than usual, we wonder, "What's all this for? I'm not enjoying this at all. I don't look forward to it. And I certainly don't find pleasure in reciting it." Then if we are lay-people we reflect there's no obligation to say the Office anyway, so why don't we concentrate on private prayer instead?

Private prayer instead! That gets just as bad: somehow God hides himself and we come reluctantly to our prayer, thinking, "I remember when I was first professed, prayer was so easy and it isn't now." I put myself in the presence of God and ten minutes later I realise that I've worked out the whole programme for next week and precisely how to cook the next meal, and I haven't started to be in the presence of God – and so we start again. And we go on and on, till at the end we realise that we haven't spent actually any time at all attending to God. It's just been a very boring period of not very constructive thought.

There must be some way of getting through to God. He must be there somewhere.... "Now, yes, if for lunch we have baked potatoes ... and we have some celery ... there's a bit of fish left over .... Yes, Lord I really do want to attend to you Lord. Yes, Lord, um, I've been here ten minutes. How much longer do you want me here Lord...?" There's nothing to hold the concentration. So then we think, "Well, perhaps at least I can pray for other people." And we wonder fretfully, "Who is there that you want me to pray for? Mrs So-and-so? Isn't she a bore! Yes, Lord I really do want to pray. Yes, I do Lord. There's nearly another minute gone."

Where has the joy been hidden? Why is it that after we have been given all that glorious fervour, all that grace, we don't seem to be getting anywhere? We're doing things exactly the same way as we did before. We go into the chapel; we use the rosary, or perhaps a book, to start us off; 'putting ourselves in the presence of God'. ("What does that mean? Aren't you here all the time, Lord? It certainly doesn't seem as if you are.") And yet there was a time when we knew precisely what we meant by 'the presence of God'. Then, of course, we begin to wonder what is the point of all this? 'Here I am wasting half an hour just sitting or kneeling, looking at my watch, wondering when on earth this is going to end. I'm really wasting my time on prayer. Aren't I Lord? I'd be much more useful if I went and did something practical: how about if I went to do some visiting for the SVP?'

And then we realise that we don't really want to visit these dreadful old people. "I mean, there's that sort of gipsy family encamped at the other end of the parish. I know that I did say that I'd go in and read to the children and get some medicines for them but, really Lord, it's awfully boring doing that. They don't really want me, Lord. Do they? Our parish visiting ... is it really worthwhile? I'm sure it's only an interruption to them. They are awfully embarrassed when I call. Wouldn't it be much better if I just stayed behind and prayed for them? Oh, I've just remembered I can't pray either. Well, whatever I do Lord, there must be something you can do, if you're there at all."

All the joy seems to have gone out of Christian work as well as Christian prayer. The joy of caring for the church, caring for the altar ... there was a time when you really enjoyed ironing purificators, sewing lace onto albs! Now it seems totally pointless, futile. "Why can't we use paper purificators, anyway?" There was a time when we really enjoyed writing letters to lonely people; when we really enjoyed cooking meals for those who couldn't look after themselves; a time when we really enjoyed visiting the hospital, going from bed to bed, spreading radiance as we went. Now we feel dreadfully embarrassed. "No, these people don't want to see me, Lord." The whole of our Christian life, our prayer, our good works, everything seems pointless.

At this stage, of course, we look with extreme irritation at those people who are still in the fervour of their first conversion, thinking how dreadfully smug they are. "How on earth can they go on kneeling there, quietly praying, when I can't? Surely they know by now that prayer doesn't work." We go on like this for a period, getting thoroughly irritable, thoroughly frustrated by everybody else ... and then all at once the sun comes through again! We suddenly recognise the experience that St Ignatius had. All right, we dread going to Mass and we don't enjoy being at Mass, but we do feel marvellous when it's all over! We dread visiting the hospital, and we feel terribly embarrassed when actually talking to people who are sick, but when we come out of the hospital we have this glorious sense of well-being. After a bit even we realise that, though we aren't looking forward to our Christian activity, and we don't enjoy it at all while we're doing it, we do feel very good indeed after it's over.

We understand, as St Ignatius understood, that this is one of the ways we can tell the will of the Lord. Sin is something that we look forward to doing, and feel bad about afterwards; a good action is something that we may dread doing, but we do feel good about afterwards. This is the way the Holy Spirit speaks to us, to confirm within us that it has truly been worthwhile. And when that gleam of sunlight breaks suddenly into our world, then all at once it begins to make sense. We remember that we were always promised that it would be a way of the Cross. We had clearly been warned that there would be a sword of sorrow. "Aren't we marvellous, we've actually endured all that for Christ!"

And so the joy comes back into our lives when we realise that all this incredibly boring, dull, dry prayer is actually something given to God. We've not gone into it for the sake of the pleasure we get out of it. We've gone into it really for the love of God and nothing else: we can take comfort in that! We can say to ourselves afterwards, "Yes, I did stick out my half-hour there, and, even if I did look at my watch from time to time, I stayed with it. And now

I can see that the grace of God is working throughout the rest of the day. And, yes, I did find the way Father said Mass extremely irritating, but the grace of the sacrament doesn't depend on that; God really is still working in my life. And, yes, maybe I didn't enjoy going round the hospital at all but it did good to other people and I feel now the reward of good works." So we realise that when we were complaining all the time, "Where is God? Why has he abandoned us? Where on earth is he? Why is he not there when things get difficult?" The answer was, of course, that he was there hidden right inside our hearts.

We realise when this burst of sunshine comes into our life that it's during these difficult moments that we're really proving our love of God. After all, if the Christian life were always easy, if it were always a pleasure to go to Mass and a pleasure to pray and a pleasure to help other people, why then we wouldn't really be doing it for the love of God at all! We would be doing it because we enjoy it, looking after our own pleasure. But now we're struggling through, doing things that are no pleasure to us. Yes, in the case of Christian works we are obviously helping other people, but in the case of our prayer and our Mass, we cannot see what good it is doing to us or anybody else. But what we're actually proving to ourselves and to other people is that we love God.

Traditionally this sort of experience is called a period of 'dryness', although my metaphor began by calling it rain! When we've come through this difficult patch, struggling up the hill through the damp and the mist, we can sit back in the evening in pleasant company, in the company of the saints and say, "Yes Lord, it wasn't pleasant at the time, and I wish you hadn't made me do it, but I do recognise now that I have some element of the love of God in my heart, and that must mean that God loves me." That is a marvellous realisation to have. After our struggle up these bleak Pyrenees we can relax in the knowledge of the love of God, and that gives us courage to continue. Of course, things don't get easier, but now we are well aware that it may be difficult; and it really is worthwhile doing something difficult for God. Yes, we don't look forward to doing Christian work, or saying our prayers, but we know that we will feel better for it later on. We have the courage to continue with a stronger and a more mature faith, in the knowledge that whenever God seems to be hiding himself, he's always right there in the temple of our heart.

The same thing, of course, happened to Our Lady and St Joseph. They took Jesus to Jerusalem for the Passover feast at the age of twelve when he became 'the son of the Law', the Bar-mitsva. And on the way back from Jerusalem they found that he was gone. Suddenly all the joy had departed from their lives. They were left wondering, "Why has he abandoned us? Where can he be?" They searched for three days, unable to find him, unable to gather any news of him, wondering what had gone wrong. "What have we done wrong? Why has all the joy departed?" The Gospel doesn't tell us all the details, but we can imagine them searching the countryside with the group that were heading back together, and then returning to the city, trailing around the streets, around the temples, perhaps even investigating the prisons and the hospitals, searching desperately and finding no joy, no pleasure, nothing but dread. They tried the bazaars, seeking cheerfully in the street of the sweet sellers, and looking with terror among the slave traders. St Joseph kept having bright ideas, but each morning came and each evening with the same emptiness and desolation.

And then they find him: they find him where they might have thought of looking for him first, right there in the Temple where he had been all the time. The joy that reawakens when they find him is a joy that reveals to them how much deeper their love is. Now their love has been proved: they know that they really love him. They spent three days searching for him. Had they not cared for him, they could have gone back to Nazareth, got on with their lives without him. But they cared; they loved him.

And they came to understand that, despite having lost him, his love was with them all the time. It was his love that pulled them back in the end, drew them back to the Temple.

So the joy that came into their hearts on finding Our Lord was much greater than if they had never lost him. They realised that because of the sorrow of losing him, they valued his love all the more. Our Lady remembered then how Simeon had said, "A sword of sorrow will pierce your own soul too." Perhaps she wondered, "Is this all he meant?" She may have thought, "This is it. I have passed my test." She pondered all these things in her heart. Jesus went down and lived with them in Nazareth.

PART II

RAIN ON THE MOUNTAINS

Chapter Six

Into the Twilight

Lying lonely in the garden,
Jesus dreads His Father's will;
All have fled or sleep, but only
Mary watches, silent, still.

It was after we had entered Spain that our pilgrimage really began to be penitential. This surprised us all, for we had imagined that we'd come through the worst we could possibly experience, on the hills in the rain and the thunderstorm. But no, we found that it got worse as we went on. The path was not well marked at the best of times, and for much of the way had become a main road heavy with lorries, so we had to resort to buses and trains to cross the plain of Castile. Spanish public transport is unbelievably harrowing. The timetables are a state secret, and there's no way of finding out where the bus goes from or when the bus will arrive. Trying to find somewhere to stay was even worse. To get anything to eat we found almost impossible. We passed through village after village where there was no shop, no café, nowhere to get anything. And there was mud, and the path was slippery under our feet, and the rain drizzled down steadily hour after hour.

There were nights when we weren't able to find anywhere under cover to sleep, so we had to camp out in the rain. I recall settling on one excessively steep hillside which sloped straight into a swift and stony stream. In the town on the other bank was a particularly noisy funfair that lasted all night – it was because of the fiesta that there had been no room for us in any possible inn. It didn't take long before we were wondering what was so very special about Compostela anyway. "Wouldn't it be much nicer to go back to France where the weather is better and we can speak the language and get on with the people?" It was at this point really that one began to feel, "I don't think I want to go any further on this beastly pilgrimage." We had to keep reminding each other of the fact that, if there was no real way back, there was certainly no way sideways either. We just had to keep going on. So we squelched on into the mist and the rain, our journey not very consoling, not very comforting. After four or five days walking in the rain, nothing was still glamorous. All the great feelings about doing something heroic for God had long since disappeared. We just had to keep on....

This happens in our spiritual life as well. There comes a time when it gets absolutely horrific, and we realise that all the difficulties we had before were nothing at all. We realise – this is perhaps the most terrifying realisation – we realise just how much God could ask of us. It's not that he has asked it yet, but he could ask. We think of all the things that he has asked of his saints. We make the mistake of reading the lives of the saints and then we stop and think, "What if I had to do that!" And we look ahead at the possibility of losing everything that we count dear, just as we already seem to have lost our joy in prayer. We don't get any pleasure from our faith; we don't find any pleasure in our Christian life, so what else is there to live for? Our Lord may be preparing to take away our friends, our homes, our health, everything. And we call out, "Why Lord? Why do we have to give up all this?" And he says simply, "Follow me. You are not worthy of me unless you take up your cross. Follow me."

At this stage the temptation is to compare ourselves with others: "Other people don't have to give up everything." As we look at people around us, we see lots of good, worthy, holy people who are living very easy lives, surrounded by all the comforts of this world and of the next. They find prayer easy and they are surrounded by friends and they have clothing and shelter and food, everything they want. "Why do you expect me to give up all that?" And the answer is, "Don't bother about them. You follow me." We think "This doesn't seem fair, Lord, because we've already done more than most people do for you. We do have a regular practice of prayer. We do receive the sacraments. We do our best to be charitable, to be kind. We are certainly doing more than other people around. Oh, yes, Lord, we are not claiming anything for ourselves. We know this is only by your grace. We are very much aware that it is only your grace that enables us to do this. But there you are Lord: haven't we done enough?" The answer is still "Deny yourself, follow me."

So then we look at all the happy pagans around us and say "Lord, Lord, really this isn't fair. Look at all those pagans, enjoying this life, doing whatever they feel like; and in the end they are all going to be saved by their invincible ignorance. Lord, why can't I be invincibly ignorant? It would be so much easier, Lord, to be a good pagan, even to be a bad pagan in blissful ignorance. It all seems so dreadfully unfair. Why have I been given this terrible gift of faith which means I know what I ought to do, this terrible gift of Christian life, which means that I've got no excuse?" We have to admit that we know too much. We can see the pagans living around us, living very comfortable lives, totally unconcerned about the things of the next world. And we can agree that they are all good and worthy people according to their lights, and that they are all going to heaven through their invincible ignorance ... but we can't go back. We can't abandon the way of the cross and simply go and live like everybody else, much as we'd like to.

There are times when we complain, "Well, Lord, maybe we can't go back but at least can't we stay still? Surely we have given enough; you can't want us to give any more." We feel terrible; the Lord doesn't seem to give any sign of consolation. There's still no joy in prayer. There's still no joy in Christian life. There remains only this persistent demand: "Stop clinging on. Deny yourself.

Follow me." It's no good looking at other people. Other people don't seem to be concerned; other people don't seem to see what the fuss is about. Yes, we do talk to other people: we consult confessors and directors, we ask our friends and companions to advise us. And they look on with total indifference and say, "I don't see what all the fuss is about. You're doing all right as it is. Just carry on. Don't worry." Are they really unaware, as they seem to be, of what it is that's really concerning us? And still we hear this relentless voice, again and again: "Don't bother about them. Follow me."

So we start trying to bargain with the Lord. "All right, Lord, I'll follow you on condition that I can join this particular religious order." The Lord says: "Don't make conditions. Follow me." "Well, I'll follow you, Lord, on condition that I can have this one special friend with me. I'll follow you Lord, as long as I can remain with my family." How often do we hear the voice of the Lord saying again, "Leave the dead to bury their dead. You follow me!" We say, "I'll follow you Lord, if you give me at least some sort of self respect, if you'll make me a great and famous preacher, if you'll make me well-known as a famous hermit or a great ascetic." But still he will not make conditions, still there is no consolation.

We can't bargain with the Lord. He has after all treated us very gently up till now, and although it doesn't seem like it now, we can remember our times of fervour, times when serving the Lord was really a pleasure and a joy. We can remember times when, even after difficulties, we were able to come up smiling and say, "Yes, Lord, we've done something marvellous for you." But our memories of all that seem to fade and we're left lying face-down in the mud, crying to the Lord, "I really don't want to go any further." And all we hear in reply is, "Follow me. Follow me."

We look around for a way out, and realise that there is no way out. Oh, of course we still have our freedom. We are free to abandon the Lord altogether, to leave the pilgrimage. And then as soon as we imagine ourselves in such a position we realise that, no, our whole being cries out against it. We could not be happy if we went back and tried to be invincibly ignorant pagans. It just wouldn't work. We realise that, and sometimes the Lord shows us a glimpse of what it might mean. So in the end there is no alternative. We are left there listening to that inexorable voice urging us on, till eventually we have to say, "All right, if you really insist, Lord, thy will be done." And even then there is no comfort, just emptiness and fear.

Our Lord himself felt this same emptiness and fear. He went out across the brook Kedron to the Garden of Gethsemane, and he saw ahead of him, not only the Passion, but, far worse than that, the way in which his Passion would be so wasted, of so little effect in so many lives. So many millions of people for whom he was about to die, and they don't care in the slightest. Beginning with Judas and going on to the end of the world, there are all those for whom his Passion will be fruitless, so that his Agony will indeed continue until the end of the world.

Our Lord sees all this, and his whole human nature revolts against it: "Father if it be thy will, let this cup pass from me." Surely to redeem the world it is not necessary to do so much. Surely one drop of Christ's blood would save my soul, half a drop.... Do we witness in the Garden of Gethsemane a titanic struggle between the human nature of Our Lord and his divine nature? The disciples really don't seem to care: there they are asleep, a stone's throw away. They can't be bothered even to watch and pray. They are not concerned; they don't understand. For Jesus there is no human comfort whatsoever.

And Our Lady, where is she? She is probably still at the Cenacle, but filled with a nameless dread. She doesn't know what is going to be, but she knows that something terrible is happening. So she remains there, perhaps with the other women, Mary the wife of Cleopas, Mary of Magdala, all of them confused, frightened, apprehensive. Something is afoot. They could tell from the expression on Our Lord's face when he left that something is proceeding, but they don't know what. So they too are facing a bleak future. We must imagine the women gathering round Mary, as she remembers once again her first prayer: "Be it done unto me according to thy word." And at the same moment her Son is kneeling in Gethsemane, and cries out, "Not as my will is but as thine is."

Chapter Seven

Under the Scourge

Blows of scourge and lash of hatred,
Bruise the flesh of God the Word:
Broken flesh of human nature,
Mary's heart pierced by the sword.

As the difficulties of our pilgrimage increased, I began to realise that being a pilgrim was not at all the same thing as being on holiday. In fact I did wonder whether I could get away with claiming a holiday after we returned to England. I didn't! What I think surprised me more than anything else was the degree of physical pain that we experienced in Spain. To begin with, my walking boots started to pinch, and eventually really began to hurt, even though they were thoroughly broken in and had never given any trouble before or since. I thought I was quite accustomed to those boots, but they began to chafe as if they were new: and of course as we walked on day after day, on rough paths, usually with wet socks, they began to chafe and hurt more and more. At last it became quite difficult to move. I had to cut a stick and hobble along the road like the original mediæval pilgrims.

Then the rucksack began to give trouble. We had all our luggage on our backs of course, and although never before or since have I had any difficulty carrying a rucksack, during that part of the pilgrimage through Spain I found the bag was pulling more and more on one shoulder until there was a permanent ache on that side. I stumbled on, hobbling from stone to stone, trying to shift the weight of the rucksack, moving it up or down, changing things round, in endless futile attempts to make it easier. It became a matter of endurance: just plodding on trying not to think about it. Then in addition most of us began to get colds or coughs of various sorts or other, with the continual rain. Eventually we realised that all of us, in one way or another, were actually having to cope with a fair amount of suffering, which is not in the least bit what we bargained for when we started on our pilgrimage.

We never do bargain for it, but as we proceed on our pilgrimage through life suffering seems to be something which comes to virtually everyone who sets out to follow Christ. The Way of the Cross was after all a way of very acute physical suffering. We should not be as surprised as we are, when we see how often God's saints are asked to bear suffering. St Teresa had to tell him once, that no wonder he has so few friends since he treats them so badly. I suppose if we are foolish enough to surrender to God, and actually to say, "Thy will be done," we should expect his first demand to be that we accept physical suffering for his sake.

Of course for some people suffering comes in the simple form of martyrdom. There are many who have been scourged, imprisoned, laden with chains, tortured, put to death, for the sake of the Gospel. And yet those who suffer physically for the sake of the faith, at the hands of those who really hate Our Lord, these real martyrs have always the consolation and the glory of knowing that at least in this they are suffering for Christ. We are told in the Acts of the Apostles that when the apostles were scourged for the first time they came away thrilled and excited at having suffered for the sake of Christ. They were glad of it, as so many martyrs since have been glad with the same exhilaration. Real martyrdom seems to be a form of physical suffering that is fairly easy to undertake.

What is much more difficult, and what far more of Our Lord's saints have been asked to bear, is a suffering with no glamour. If we are physically attacked by other people we cannot comfort ourselves by reflecting that it is for the sake of the Gospel, or for the faith or anything, if it is a purely arbitrary attack, or merely in the course of robbery. There have been a number of holy people who have suffered at the hands of wicked men but without the consolation of thinking, "Well at least they've attacked me because I'm a priest, or because I'm a Christian." Those two strange twentieth-century hermits, Charles de Foucauld and John Bradburne, were both eventually killed in a way totally irrelevant to their faith and their witness. They were hauled away in the middle of the night, beaten and put to death, but not because they were Christians, faithful witnesses to God: in both cases it was only an irrelevant skirmish at the end of a war. There was none of the glamour of martyrdom, only a sense of suffering unjustly, without reason or for the wrong reason. (Charles de Foucauld has since been beatified, but not as a martyr.)

Then for so many, for so very many of God's people, suffering has taken the form of physical sickness. We remember how St Teresa, when she was a novice, was foolish enough to say, as she tended a sick nun, "I hope I shall be able to bear such great suffering for the sake of Christ." And Our Lord turned round almost at once and allowed her to suffer very great sickness indeed, so that they despaired of her life. Even when she had recovered from that, the rest of her life was a succession of sicknesses and injuries. She was the sort of chronic invalid that would certainly never have been admitted to a convent these days, because if it wasn't one thing it was another. If the climate in one place was bad for her, somewhere else it was even worse. Even in her home town she exclaimed how extraordinary it was that she couldn't cope with the climate, despite having been born there. She would have quartan fevers, tertian fevers and quinzy fevers in confusing succession. And then eventually, you remember, she broke her arm and it refused to mend: she really had a lifetime of physical suffering!

Many of the other saints have gone through the same sort of thing. Sometimes a new convert in the first flush of enthusiasm is liable to say something like, "Since the power of God casts out sickness, a real Christian can never be sick," and they despise these weak Christians in their illness. Yet we only have to look at the lives of the saints to see how far that is from being the truth. Suffering does seem to be part of our birthright as Christians. We are after all on the Way of the Cross, and the suffering of the body, physical suffering, is something that Our Lord asks the majority of his people to carry. Our physical life on this earth becomes nothing but a weariness, and we cry out to be released and to be with God. We can hear this in the Old Testament, in the Psalms. We can hear it in the New Testament, where St Paul complains about the suffering he's had to endure, being scourged, being ship-wrecked, in danger from robbers, in danger from rivers, in danger from storms, continually suffering, but aware that he is at one with Christ in that suffering.

When we ask what the point of it all is, Our Lord doesn't always give us an answer. Sometimes even the saints are provoked to anger against him, exclaiming, "How dare you treat me like this?" And the Lord gives no consoling answers whatsoever. St Teresa once commented that life seemed to be one perpetual "Bad night in a bad inn." (I think I know precisely the Spanish inn she was thinking about.) And yet that is the path of the Cross, the path of Christ, one of perpetual suffering. Why is that? It can only be to put Brother Ass in his place, to remind us that this world and everything in it is passing. There is nothing in this world that doesn't decay. The most glorious and the most beautiful things created on this earth are only transitory. Perhaps the most beautiful things we ever see are the wild flowers on the hills, and look, they last only a few days. The glorious glittering dragonfly lives no more than a day or so. The most dazzling things in God's creation, radiant in all their splendour and their glory, only go to feed the oxen tomorrow, as Our Lord puts it.

So it is with our own souls, our own lives, our own bodies: we are born into a world where everything comes into being and passes away. Part of the process of coming close to Christ seems to be recognising how frail this material world is; how although it is a thing of great beauty, that beauty is essentially transient. We cannot hold on to anything in this world, whether it's physical health, or material possessions, whether it's the beauty of the world around us, or the beauty in our own lives. All this passes away. God seems to be determined to make sure that all his friends realise that. Some people seem to get away without this experience, but those who are called closer to God, closer to a life of prayer, in some way or another always seem to have to bear this breakdown of the flesh. It may be a long and weary struggle, or it may be only a short time of anguish. Some people go through a period of great pain and sickness and then come back to health; for others illness seems to be a lifelong vocation. But for nearly everyone there is a call to accept suffering.

That is why the Church has a long established tradition of welcoming suffering voluntarily, taking on the constant little mortifications of daily life with joy, and often choosing not to take the softest option. This is not because we despise the good things that God has given us, but in order to prepare ourselves for the probability of sharing the suffering of the Cross. Some of the confessors of the faith have told us how effective this voluntary internal mortification can be. There was an American Jesuit called Walter Ciszek who was imprisoned for thirty years in the Soviet Union: he says that he was able to cope with the conditions in prison because of the discipline of his Jesuit noviciate, the voluntary acts of self-denial, the fasting, the sleeplessness, the long hours of prayer. He was able to retain his faith and even exercise his priesthood until eventually he was released.

Because of this there is a danger of thinking that physical suffering is a good thing in itself. It isn't of course: it is an evil, just as the Cross was an evil. And yet the Cross has become the sign of our glory and our triumph. We may well have to cope with physical suffering, but it isn't something that God actually wills for us. It's something that God permits in order that we can progress to a greater good. We should always remember that God does not desire that we should suffer. Our Lord did not desire suffering for himself: he accepted it, and we likewise accept suffering because of a greater good that is to come. And yet suffering wouldn't really be suffering if we could see that greater good. That is the difference perhaps between real martyrdom and the daily martyrdom of sickness. The martyr on the scaffold can immediately see the glory that is to come. The martyr confined by sickness cannot see the point and therefore the suffering is the greater and the more intense.

Our Lord was scourged at the pillar. The Gospels tell us no details about it, but the archæologists and painters give us ample food for the imagination. Our Lord's scourging was a pointless and irrelevant part of his Passion. Pontius Pilate said, "I find this man innocent. Therefore I will scourge him and then let him go free": the most absurd and irrational judgement! If Pilate had really thought him guilty, then the scourging was an irrelevance; Our Lord should have gone straight to the Cross. So the scourging at the pillar was an unnecessary extra, but none the less terrible. What happened at the pillar was the bruising and the breaking of the flesh, the Flesh which the Word had taken on.

The scourging of Christ was a direct contradiction of the Incarnation. In the womb of Mary the Word was made Flesh, but now that body of Christ, the body of Christ that we worship, is broken, bruised and torn apart by the scourging. It is the last attempt by Satan to undo the work of the Incarnation, as if Satan is trying to reverse what God achieved when Jesus was born, trying to break apart that union between the Word and the Flesh.

Satan of course failed, and Our Lord accepted the suffering, very severe physical suffering, in his human body. But for Our Lady too there was suffering. She can't have been present; maybe she heard what was going on, or maybe she only learnt of it afterwards. But in any case the flesh that was being bruised was her flesh too, because Jesus took flesh from the body of Mary. In the scourging of Our Lord, Our Lady too is suffering. And we remember that in the Christian life we are all together, no member of the Church can suffer without the rest of us suffering, because we are all one body, one spirit in Christ.

Chapter Eight

Despised and Rejected

Thorn-encircled head enduring
Mocking, shocking shouts of hate:
Peter's fear denies his Master;
Only Mary still can wait.

One point that became very obvious as we were walking through Spain was that eight is a bad number. If there had been fifty of us we would have clearly needed a recognised leader, so that when the leader said "Move" everyone would have moved. We would have taken it for granted that a big group needs organisation, a plan and a timetable. Whereas if there had been only three or four of us, we could have decided as we went along how fast we were going to go, where we were going to stop and so on. A group of eight, neither one thing nor t'other, really didn't work. There weren't enough for us to need a leader and there were too many to be casual about it. As a result by the time we were half way to Compostela we were beginning to get very bored with each other's company and at times members of the group became extremely difficult. There were those that wanted to walk faster than the others, and there were those that wanted to walk slower. Sometimes the same people would do first one then the other. There were those who would lag behind infuriatingly slowly when the rain was at its heaviest and we were pressing on to get to some sort of shelter. And then there were those who would manage to disappear just at the wrong moment. Typically this would be at the end of a lunch stop, when everybody had just struggled into their rucksacks, and suddenly we would notice that someone was missing. People would wander off into a town and start looking round the shops just when we were expecting a rare bus. There were all sorts of difficulties. There was one who persistently refused to join in the community prayers at any stage. There was another one who was happy with the prayers but didn't seem to want any food, and would sit outside in the rain while the rest of us were in a café facing the choice of tripe or octopus. Well, perhaps he had a point there! We realised that among the many obstacles in life other people can be the greatest.

It's certainly like that in our Christian pilgrimage. Sometimes we feel it would be so much easier if God allowed us to be solitary pilgrims on our own. But, no, as we realised when thinking about the Visitation, God calls us to walk together on our pilgrimage. He chooses companions for us; and it often turns out that they're really not the sort of people we like to be with at all. Everyone on the path to sanctity has to learn to cope with difficult people. That is not to say that they are wicked or evil people. Those would not be a problem, for we expect the wicked to be difficult, and we find it rather flattering when they are. If we are attacked by people who are obviously the minions of Satan, it can be quite exhilarating to know that we are important enough to be worth attacking. Opposition from the groundlings can be very annoying, but, when we stop to think about it, we become, if anything, rather proud of it. If the wicked of this world, those who are opposed to the faith and every part of it, attack us verbally or in other ways, well, that's only what we should expect. That's easy to deal with.

The difficulty comes when we find we're attacked by good people, as we will be sooner or later, if we're really going to follow Christ. We can be misunderstood by very holy people: that is much more difficult to deal with. If a narrowboat full of ravaging Vikings comes up the river to slaughter the community with fire and sword, you can take that with equanimity. That's part of being a Christian. But when a good and very holy bishop decides to try to suppress the community or destroy its work, then you do have difficulties. That has been the experience of the saints right from the beginning: they suffered most opposition from people within the Church, from people who had dedicated their whole lives to God, from people who were fundamentally good, despite being fundamentally mistaken.

If we read the authentic lives of the saints, in almost all of them we find some story of a clash with ecclesiastical authority. That was often the most difficult thing they had to endure. Many saints were excommunicated at some time of their life, some of them several times. St Thomas Aquinas was suspected of heresy, and after his death even condemned; St Thomas of Hereford and St Joan of Arc actually died excommunicated. There were clashes with bishops and archbishops, even with Popes. Saints and those near to sainthood have had to struggle against great opposition from precisely the sort of people that you might have thought would have been on their side. Think of Savonarola in his attempt to reform the morals of the city of Florence: all went well until the Pope intervened and tried to stop him. Think of so many of the great religious founders; the obstacles that were put in the way of St Francis, or even, in the very early days, the opposition to St Benedict himself. He was poisoned by his first monks, hounded out of Subiaco and driven off to Monte Cassino. Not by the barbarians – the savage King Tottila came and knelt at his feet and asked for instruction – no, it was monks and bishops who made life unpleasant for St Benedict. And then of course we remember how St John of the Cross and St Teresa had more than their share of opposition from bishops, from papal nuncios, from the inquisition, from provincials and vice-provincials, and from every sort of ecclesiastical authority.

None of these persecutors were wicked people: they were in their own ways good and holy, striving to do their best to serve God. Yet somehow in their service of God they created purgatory for others who were in the same service: a purgatory that was very difficult to endure because part of sanctity is of course self-doubt. One of the greatest trials that St Teresa had to bear was knowing that she was on her own and that at times all ecclesiastical authority, all her confessors and the best spiritual directors, agreed that she was totally wrong. Her confessors told her that all her lights in prayer were delusions of the devil; she was told to drive away the image of Christ with the sign of the cross and a contemptuous gesture. She was racked with doubt, knowing in herself the truth of God's grace, yet knowing as well that legitimate ecclesiastical authority said it was not true.

Along with opposition goes mockery and scorn, disparagement of one sort or another. So often it happens that the saints entrust their secrets to good and holy people who immediately promulgate them to the world, putting the worst possible light on them. Those who have felt called to the depths of prayer find themselves ridiculed by holy people who are simply unable to understand them. And nearly always those who were called to reform the Church have been attacked, ridiculed, slandered in every conceivable way. The great reforming saints, such as Gregory VII or Charles Borromeo, led lives of continual struggle. Not against wicked people, for these fell onto their knees and were converted: the struggle was always against clergy, against religious, against people who were genuinely trying to be good. Was it not a priest who tried to assassinate St John Bosco?

It's always the best of people with the best of intentions that make life so difficult for the saints. St John Vianney was extremely unpopular with clergy – and they were good clergy on the whole. They thought he was really unfit to be ordained and shouldn't on any account be allowed to hear confessions. Then, as the crowds began to gather, all the local clergy began to put out rumours against him. Women would wander up and down the streets crying, "That man is the father of my child." Every possible slander, every possible mockery, every possible disgrace, was loaded on the heads of the saints.

And even those quiet, hidden saints, who don't get involved

in public life, have had the same opposition from good people, being misunderstood. St Thérèse of Lisieux talks about how things that she did, and things that she said, were misunderstood within the community, yet not maliciously. That is the way that it always seems to be. It is a difficult cross to bear because, as I said, we are so far from certain of our own perfection that, when good people are opposing us, our first instinct is to think they're right. Perhaps all we are trying to do is self-delusion, putting ourselves forward. Wouldn't it be much better just to go along with everybody else? Certainly that was the temptation put in the path of the great reformers. Wouldn't it be so much easier just to be content with Christian life as everyone else does it? Why should you want to go off and found a special sort of convent? What's wrong with the convent you're in at the moment? Isn't it spiritual pride trying to start a reform? All these temptations come in again and again! And there is no tangible experience of grace to keep us going, only a deep-rooted feeling of determination, of vocation, "We must keep going, we cannot give in!" Somehow I have to follow my call, keep on my path of pilgrimage. This path of prayer, this path of reform, whatever it is, is what I have to do, and I know that if I do give in, I shall be untrue to myself.

All this would be easy to cope with if it happened in a time of enlightenment during prayer, but it is very hard indeed to handle it at times when the Lord is hiding his face and we are left on our own, wondering whether to go on being obstinate and pig-headed, in opposition to the advice of all these good and holy people. It is a very hard part of the Passion to emulate: and yet it does seem to be something which Our Lord asks of so very many people.

After all, this is something that Jesus himself experienced, for he was mocked and jeered at, crowned with thorns. Some of the scorners, some of the soldiers who were actually mocking him, might have been there in the crowd only a few days before, shouting "Hosanna!" They were not bad people on the whole, not wicked people, but they were carried away on a wave of common feeling, joining in with what everyone else is doing, mocking this person who was claiming to be the King of the Jews. After all, the Jewish authorities all agreed he couldn't possibly be the King of the Jews, and they ought to know! The chief priests, the elders and the scribes and the Pharisees, these were good people, who had dedicated their whole lives to the service of God. The scribes and the Pharisees were precisely those who were so much in love with God that everything they did, every moment of every day, was dedicated to thinking about God. And these were the people who were jeering at Our Lord: these were the people who whipped up the crowd to shout for Barabbas: these were the people who denounced him as a fraud. It was good people who led the mockery and the jeers and the shouts.

Our Lord of course was confident and knew the truth about himself and his mission, but the same was not true for the disciples and even Our Lady: they were outside, perhaps, hearing the mockery. The jeers must have spread through the city. What can the disciples have thought? "Here is this unique man that we've been following from Galilee, and now all the leaders of our faith, the chief priests the scribes the Pharisees and the elders, they are all telling us that he's not good. They're laughing at him. What then are we to believe?"

It must have been a great trial of faith for all the apostles and Our Lady as well. Maybe she can remember the night when the angels sang at Bethlehem; but the memory is faint now. All she can hear are the jeers and the curses and the blows. She may have heard the shouts which accompanied the Crowning with Thorns. Perhaps she was even there when Pilate brought him out and said, "This is the man," and heard the crowd howling for the Blood of her Son.

Chapter Nine

The Long Trudge

On the road to desolation
Jesus bears his cross, his pain.
Mary meets him, wracked with anguish,
Sorrow wounds her heart again.

Considering that people have been walking to Compostela for thousands of years, you might think that the path would by now be well-marked. But no, it isn't. There was supposed to be a marked footpath to keep us off the main roads away from the lorries, leading more or less in a straight line across Spain from Roncesvalles to Compostela, but the way-marking was of very variable quality. In fact I believe in the Middle Ages there wasn't really a single path, but rather a general direction that people wandered: not all the pilgrimage churches are on the same line and you can't visit them all without zigzagging. Now there is an agreed route, and in the French sector this had been very well maintained; there were nice little way-marks in red, white and yellow, and at every possible turning a sign to show you where to go.

When we got to the Spanish side we found that they were not so enthusiastic about marking the path. There were supposed to be yellow arrows and we began to be somewhat obsessed with looking for these yellow arrows which sometimes led us on our way and sometimes not. At times the path would run between two stone walls, and there they painted a beautiful yellow arrow every yard: it is very easy to paint on stone walls. But then the path would come out into a marsh with nothing but heather and weeds: there wasn't anything to paint yellow arrows on, so they didn't try. There we would be with rabbit tracks going off in fifteen directions, and no idea which one was the road to Compostela. More than once we found that we'd wandered a long way off the path, and had to traverse backwards and forwards across the countryside in search of the evasive yellow arrows.

The other problem we found in Spain was the inaccuracy of the maps: the idea seemed to be that they marked villages more or less in the right places, but connecting roads were just drawn straight, without indicating how the road wriggled and wandered across mountains and marshes, ravines and streams. Looking at the map we might think it's only about three miles to the next village, and only after we'd walked about twenty miles would we realise that the path was a great deal more wiggly than the map implied. It meant that we never knew how far we had to go. If we strayed onto the main road there'd be regular signposts saying 'Camino de Santiago', and giving the distance to Compostela in kilometres, but the main road was a narrow one with heavy lorries going in both directions, so we were forced again to get off the road onto the yellow-arrowed and labyrinthine paths.

We had no idea how far we had to go. Even if our immediate goal was no further than the next village, we knew not how long it would take to get there. Sometimes what should have been quite a short easy day's walk turned out to be a long trek, taking us from seven in the morning till after dark. Distances seemed to vary enormously, as did people's estimates of how many days more walking lay before us: a few days? or several weeks? Few of the locals had ever dreamed of walking the way we were going, and fewer really knew how far we would have to go. There were some landmarks, big towns or well-known monasteries, but in between we really had no idea how far we had come or where we were on the map. All we could do was trudge on, hoping at least for an eventual change of scenery or a break in the steady drizzle.

It would be so very nice if we had accurate and detailed maps for the spiritual life! It would be lovely to be able to know that we had got to such and such a point, and tomorrow would get to the next, and next week further on still. Or to be assured that whatever difficulties we have today will certainly be passed by next week. We feel that if there were a set timetable, it would be quite easy to cope with all these difficulties. Yes, we could bear the misunderstanding and the slander by all our friends because we know it will only last a few days, and then they'll be on our side; or we can endure physical suffering because we know it is only scheduled for so many hours or days. But it isn't like that, is it? If we are asked to suffer in the Lord's service, we don't know how long that will go on. Or, if we are enjoying the peace of the Lord's service, we don't know how long that will go on either. All we can do really is to enjoy time as it passes, in what has been dubbed the 'sacrament of the present moment'; to enjoy it or to endure it.

Of course many people have given us maps or charts for our spiritual life. St John Cassian and St Benedict enumerate the twelve steps of the Ladder of Humility, which were elaborated by St John Climacus and St Bernard. There are the seven Mansions of St Teresa, and the various verses of the *Spiritual Canticle* of St John of the Cross. It seems so simple to use one of these schemes as a map, and to chart our own progress in advance. If only we could say, "This morning I have reached stanza number twenty-eight of the *Spiritual Canticle* and, with any luck, by the eighth of next month I'll be onto stanza twenty-nine!" (Though someone is bound to ask whether we mean the first redaction or the second, for St John wrote the book twice in different orders.) Even if we try to fix our position without timing it, deciding whether we are in the first mansion or the fourth, we find that it doesn't work. You can't fit the different schemes together, or correlate one writer's stages in prayer with another's, still less can you pinpoint your own position. St John's stanzas or Nights do not fit neatly alongside St Teresa's Mansions, however close these two saints were in life. Other writers are even less easy to put into parallel schemes: Cassian and Climacus, St Benedict and St Bernard, Richard of St Victor, Augustine Baker: they all have their way of describing advance in the spiritual life, and none of them are the same.

One might be tempted to think that perhaps one of them is right and the others all wrong, but no, if we go back and re-read all these authors we can see that they're not trying to give us a chronological history of our life as it's going to be. What they do is to indicate different aspects of progress in the spiritual life, and most of them are at pains to point out that we don't always go in the same order. On these 'ladders' and 'mountain paths' we can go up and down, backwards, forwards and sideways and occasionally round and round in spirals. Sometimes we experience something of the seventh Mansion when really we know perfectly well we're in the first. We can get anticipations of higher stages of prayer. We can still find echoes and reminders of the very lowest. There are times when we think we're doing quite well and then something happens to make us aware that really we haven't started at all. Charts and maps of the spiritual life are useful and all quite compatible with each other only as long as we remember that we can't ever draw out a little diagram, like the drawing at the front of *The Dark Night of the Soul*, stick a pin in it and say, "Now I'm precisely that far up the spiritual mountain."

But it doesn't work like that. We don't ever know how far we've got. Sometimes we say, "I think I've made progress in the spiritual life," and then our sensible director responds, "Well, that proves that you haven't!" If all we can say is, "I haven't got anywhere yet but I'm starting again today," that's often a very good sign. Father Faber somewhere gives some guidelines for how to know if you're doing well, and says one of the important signs is to feel that you're continually having to make a completely new start. We do: we have to keep making new starts. And as well as that, we can recognise when the Lord has given us certain graces, and we can be aware that we've persevered despite the difficulties of prayer for some period of time. We can tell at least whether we've been faithful to our times of prayer and to the Divine Office. At least we've done that! We may not have had any great feelings or emotions or thoughts during our prayer, and it may well have been a time of sitting there blankly staring at the hourglass, but at least we've given that time ... and then we have to remember again that we've only just started.

Some who are just beginning seem to get ahead of us very quickly: but then some people go through life very much quicker than others. We only need think of St Thérèse of Lisieux: she got away with a very short path to perfection. Others have to struggle on for many years longer. Nor do we know how long each phase of our spiritual life is going to last. We can only acknowledge that whatever state we're in now is not permanent. The Lord is certainly going to ask us to move on, to develop, to grow. We'll never get to the point where the Lord will say to us, "All right, I've got you to precisely where I want you. You needn't change again, you're perfect now." That certainly won't happen in this life. Whatever state we're in now, whether it's a state of joy or a state of desolation, we can be sure that at some time God is going to ask us to go further. We don't know quite what's coming next, and we certainly don't know when.

One of the difficulties is that sometimes these phases seem to last an extraordinarily long time, sometimes twenty or thirty years without moving. Some of the saints talk about amazingly long periods of dryness and desolation in prayer. Others seem to have enjoyed the presence of God and a real feeling of joy for equally long. There have been saints who have had daily visions for a period of many years. But then sometimes a phase goes very quickly indeed and all we can say is, "Yes, there was a moment when I had a glimpse of the joy of the Lord. But that lasted about five minutes; I am now back in desolation." You can't tell, you can't tell. All one can do is just live in the present moment and say, "This is where I am now, and I want the Lord to lead me where he would have me be. I don't know how to do it but he knows."

The little book of extracts from Père Grou called *How to Pray* gives the same title to all the first five chapters: 'Only God can teach us to pray'. That is to emphasise that we can't make our own little pattern in life, we can't decide, "I've got so far, tomorrow I'm going to go so much further." We have to let God lead us, and sometimes he does seem to lead us round and round in circles, or on occasion apparently he doesn't lead us anywhere at all. Sometimes it looks as if he's leading us right out of the way, but all we have to do is trust him and follow him. He may show us a yellow arrow from time to time to let us know we're on the right path. Very often he seems to leave us without the yellow arrows. We just have to keep going, trusting somehow that God knows what he's doing. It may be a long time. It may be a time without any real guidance and yet God is there. Somewhere underneath the mud there is a yellow arrow. Hidden somewhere in the background there is some sort of signpost. There is a guide.

Sheer endurance in the spiritual life is one of the great virtues. St Paul speaks often about endurance, just holding on, keeping going. I remember once talking to a Carthusian prior about the difficulties of the young monks. He said that the problem was that they got accustomed to having a programme of events to look forward to. You know the sort of thing: postulancy, noviciate, simple profession, solemn profession. Then for monks there's ordination to diaconate and finally priesthood, which at least the nuns are spared. But it means that from the moment of entering the monastery there is a set pattern, almost an exact timetable. You know once you're clothed as a novice that in almost exactly seven years' time you'll be ordained priest and before that there's all the study to do, exams and essays to write. But then once ordained the new priest is suddenly left to himself with nothing further to expect. That, said the prior, is when the real difficulties began, when they had to begin to live the life without further excitements, just plodding on from year to year. It is the same for any religious, monk, friar or nun. It is very similar for the secular priest: years of stressful training, and then real life at last, and no more comforting milestones to look forward to.

The difficulty is actually living the Christian life once all the preparation is over. The new convert has the excitement of months of regular instruction, visits to the presbytery, perhaps the ceremonies of the catechumenate, the process of starting a new way of life: and then after confirmation it's all over, no more stages or rites of initiation, but you have to begin to live the Christian life like everyone else. There are no more stages to reach. We have to learn to live quietly, to abide in the presence of God, to be still and simple before him.

That is something we all have to do in the spiritual life, to learn how to be still and to know that he is God. When our Lord set out to carry the Cross I don't suppose Pontius Pilate bothered to tell him where they were going or how far it would be.... They set out through the crowded streets of Jerusalem ... out through one of the gates ... into what we're told was a tangled area of old quarries and pits. The hill of Calvary itself was simply a lump of rock left surrounded by quarries: not an obvious place to be going to. Certainly it can't have been clear to the crowd, to Our Lady, to any of those following, how far our Lord was being taken, or which route they were going to take. It was just a question of trudging on. Simon of Cyrene is made to help carry the Cross, but he too doesn't know how far it's going to be. Are they going just outside the gate? Are they going well away from the city? He doesn't know. And we as well, carrying the Cross, following our Lord behind the Cross, we don't know how far it's going to be.

What then of Our Lady? She may or may not have been able to see him when he was exposed on the Lithostrotos. Certainly we believe that she met him on the road to Calvary; somewhere on this tangled road she was able to push her way through the crowd, somewhere she was able to see him but they could not speak. The crowd was moving on, the soldiers were pressing, and from there to Golgotha she had to follow somehow on the edge of the crowd, trying to keep in sight. Again and again she was crushed against the roadside, against the houses, pushed out of the way, beaten back in the crowd and then she pushed her way forward again, not knowing how far she would have to go. She didn't know how long her Way of the Cross was going to be. She had no thoughts or feelings of what was going to come next. It was only a question of holding on, holding firm, being faithful, being with him.

Chapter Ten

Darkness Falls

From the cross the pinioned Saviour
Liberates the dying thief:
God is dead – can the beloved
John support that mother's grief?

Towards the end our pilgrimage began to take on something of the nature of purgatory. There came a time when there was nothing really left to enjoy in it whatsoever. The countryside remained dull and bleak – what we could see of it through the rain and mist. The road remained badly marked, rough and stony, or noisy and full of lorries. There was nowhere to stay. We slept in ruins or half-finished buildings. We ran short of food. The choice remained boiled octopus or tripe, in the few places that would sell food; otherwise it was goat's cheese and sour wine. The company straggled so that we were hardly in touch with each other during the day and there didn't seem to be any way to escape.

There were no friendly buses or trains to take us home. We couldn't even drop out of the pilgrimage. We just had to keep going without even remembering why we thought we wanted to start. We couldn't really see any point in going to Compostela. We certainly couldn't remember anything of the joy we'd had when we started. It seemed to be a totally desolating experience with nothing to look forward to and nothing to look back at. All we could do was to endure and to exist.

There comes a time in many people's spiritual life which is like that. There is no longer any joy whatsoever. We remember perhaps that we were once rash enough to say to God, "Thy will be done," and we have seen him gradually strip away all the things in which we had taken pleasure: our friends, the joy of the Mass, the joy of our Christian work, everything seemed to go. He accepted our sacrifice, which was the last thing we really wanted when we so blithely offered it. We said to Our Lord cheerfully, "Receive my heart, my soul, my mind, everything"; but when he takes us at his word and really does receive them, we find ourselves unable to endure it. Because when we said to the Lord, "Take everything," we surely didn't mean it. We meant at least, "Remain with me, and show me that you're there. Show me how much you care." But he takes that away as well. It is the removal of the presence of God, or the feeling of the presence of God, that is the most difficult thing of all.

There comes a time when we no longer get any feeling of pleasure or enjoyment or profit out of the Mass, out of our prayer, out of our Christian work, even when we look back on it. If you remember, the first time prayer began to get difficult we found that we dreaded beginning to pray, but after we'd finished we realised the point of it. We found that we dreaded visiting the sick or attending Mass but after it was all over we felt that it had been worthwhile, there was a joy in it. But now there comes a time when we don't feel that at all, after the Mass, even after receiving Communion. We feel absolutely nothing. If anything there is a revulsion against all the things of God, a revulsion against the things of earth as well. We no longer find any pleasure in recreation, sports, reading, whatever it is that we thought we might do to get away from God. There doesn't seem to be any escape.

There comes a time when every morning is something to dread: the prospect of having to pray, having to force ourselves to give time to a God who doesn't seem to be there, doesn't seem to care, doesn't seem to listen. And when it's all over we rise from our knees feeling even worse than when we started. A time when even if we do drag ourselves out to look after someone else, or to do something for someone else, we come away from them feeling embarrassed and ashamed, wondering whether we'd have done much better to leave them alone. The Lord does sometimes accept this total sacrifice of everything, of all created good things, though mercifully not from everyone. But everyone has to be prepared to face the appalling possibility that God may well ask us to give up no less than the whole of creation. That even includes created grace, it includes all the things we've got used to thinking of as the fruits of prayer, all the things that St Paul speaks of – joy and love and peace. They all seem to go. If we try to remember them, or our friends try to remind us of how joyful things were when we started, we can only think, "Well, yes I can remember saying at the time that I enjoyed my faith, but I can't really have meant it. I was young then. I was naive. I didn't know what was happening. It was all in the mind. I made it up as I went along...."

We find that we no longer believe in our own past grace. We are left as it were stripped of everything, bare before God, though God doesn't seem to be there any more. The great saints of the past often came to a conviction that, though God might indeed be there, he had turned his face away, and in fact they were condemned, already condemned to hell: many of them speak of seeing visions of their own place in hell, with a conviction, a real certainty that there was no possibility of salvation for them. These days that doesn't seem to happen so much. Far more common now is the emptier conviction that there is no hell, no God, no heaven, that the whole of our faith, the whole of our religion is completely imaginary. One can get into the state of what has been called virtual atheism, the realisation that, here we are, spending hours in prayer, going though the motions of being a Christian, going through the motions of going to Mass, and yet we don't really believe there is a God at all.

We can find ourselves terribly challenged by this total lack of belief in God, this lack of faith. You remember how St Thérèse of Lisieux felt this. Everything that we have formerly thought so certain now seems completely uncertain. We go back and look at all the things we used to celebrate as the proofs of the love of God: the pattern and order in the universe, the beauty of creation, the variety of flowers and birds, all the things which in the past we thought so obviously proved God was with us; and now we find they don't convince us at all. Even thinking back to the moments of grace in our own lives, even if we've experienced miracles, we look back and we think, "No, it wasn't true. It can't be so." And we can find ourselves in agony as we come to believe that we have no faith at all. We don't believe in God. There is no God. So why are we going through all the motions of prayer and why are we performing the sacrifice?

Then there comes a time of real anger and frustration as we think, "I've wasted so much of my life following this dream. I've wasted the best years of my youth, giving myself to prayer and sacraments for a God that doesn't exist." And then we can become very angry indeed, angry with God for not existing. (Logic does not always survive either at this stage!) We feel nothing but emptiness and frustration, and fear of what is to come. Especially when we realise that, even if it really isn't true, and we are now able to stop all this pretence at being a Christian, it's too late to enjoy all the good things of this life. Younger people still have them, but we've left it too late for ourselves, we've given ourselves away too much!

The strange thing is that during this time of complete emptiness we are never actually able to give up prayer. We're never actually able to do without the Mass. If in the very worst moment of thinking, "I can't possibly endure to attend to this Mass" the suggestion was made, "Well, in that case, why bother?" somehow we can't get away. It's so deeply ingrained in us that the practice of the faith is something we must do, even when we feel that this time we are about to spend in mental prayer will be a complete and absolute waste of time for us and for everybody else. The idea of missing it altogether just doesn't seem possible. When we notice this, our frustration and anger can become even greater, at this God who refuses to exist. We find ourselves desolate, and in our desolation we are convinced that there is no God. So because of that we cry out to God for help.

This moment of total darkness is of course a sharing in the suffering of Our Lord on the Cross. We cannot imagine what happens in the mind of Christ. We can't presume to look into anybody else's mind, let alone the mind of the one who is both God and man. Yet somehow the humanity of Christ became totally desolate in the same way that some of the saints have been desolate: this total emptiness of prayer. We are witnessing the humanity of Christ, almost as if there was a separation for a moment between his humanity and his divinity, almost as if the perfect man, Jesus Christ, was no longer in touch with his Godhead. We cannot guess what that can mean, and yet he does seem to have experienced the very worst of what we can experience in desolation. "My God, my God, why hast thou forsaken me?"

He hangs on the Cross, unable to get away, unable to stop loving. His remaining few words from the Cross are all words of love and of forgiveness and of consolation. And yet he hangs there in total darkness and desolation. Our Lady stands at the foot of the Cross; she too must have felt this total emptiness of soul. She hears the muttered words, "Behold your son!" She feels St John take her in his arms.... "Behold your mother!" In the numbness and the shock of what is happening she can do no more than give a bare mental assent. Certainly at that moment she could not look forward to the role of being Mother of the Church. All she was conscious of was the total emptiness of her life, as the Son for whom she has lived, for whom she has given everything, her Son is being snatched from her.

Our Lady stands empty at the foot of the Cross, with St John, with St Mary Magdalene and the others, unable to pray, unable to think in terms of hope or looking forward to anything, just being there, holding on to each other, holding on to the foot of the Cross.

PART III

GLORY AT THE WORLD'S END

Chapter Eleven

Mount Joy

Empty tomb gives silent witness;
Show us, Mary, show your Son!
Death defeated, life uplifted;
Hail! Christ risen, warfare won!

There came at last a morning when, following the yellow arrows, we found ourselves climbing gently up to the top of a little green hill. The company had rather straggled by then; only one was with me. We got to the top of this hill and there was a pile of stones on the top and a bare cross stuck in the stones. We passed the cross and looked down: there below us was a little valley, and a stream trickling through it. On the other side rose the city of Santiago. There stood the towers of the cathedral, the two great baroque towers of the Obradoiro, fantastic, lacy stonework shining in the centre of the city, and all the church spires and the monasteries and houses gathered round and enclosed by the city wall. All were still wet with the morning dew, so that they glistened and sparkled in the sunlight.

All we did was sit there for a time on the grass looking out towards the holy city. We remembered the last signpost we'd seen, by the last yellow arrow, pointing up and naming Monte de Gozo, 'Mount Joy'. This was the cry – it became something of a watchword in Europe – after so many pilgrims had walked for so many days and weeks, and finally reached Mount Joy and looked across to see the city of Santiago. 'Mount Joy'!

When we break out of the dark night of our lives we are amazed at how very gently the Lord treats us. Just at the time when our spiritual life seems to be at its very worst, suddenly we realise that it has changed: joy has been reborn. For a time we hardly even notice it's happened, so little did we expect it. We were so used to being gloomy and depressed, to our prayer being a penance and a grief, that it comes as a surprise when we suddenly realise that it is no longer like that, perhaps already hasn't been so for a day or so already.

What has happened? We're almost inclined to say "What's gone wrong?" so attached are we to our sorrow and our grief and our desolation. But the light has come back into our lives and it has come so very quietly, like the dawning of a bright spring day. It doesn't come all in a moment. We don't go suddenly from total darkness to total light. But we become aware that we are able to see things again, that shadows are forming, there are now patches of sunlight, and gradually the sun rises to its full splendour. The day has come: the darkness is over. And there is something quite new about it. We are not just put back to where we were in our first fervour. Thank God for that! Our new joy is something much deeper, much more profound, the joy of glory. We are no longer quite so bouncy and ebullient in our faith, but much more profound, much more tranquil. We realise that the joys we felt in the first fervour of conversion were only a shadow or a foretaste of what we experience now. Now our prayer becomes something more intimate, a loving encounter with the bridegroom of my soul! It is the same with our Mass, our worship: we are no longer concerned about the actual form of the Liturgy. We enjoy whatever the Lord places before us. But there is a much greater depth in our sense of receiving the Lord in the sacraments. Our Christian life too is much more profound. We no longer feel quite so self-conscious about our good works, but find we can love, and do practical things in our love, much more gently. We don't have to stop and think about them.

The reawakening of joy is something impossible to describe. Other people might ask what's going on, and we are not able to say, but somehow we realise that Christ has been loving us all along. He really is there and we now understand what we mean by the love of God: Christ has risen again in my soul! We can look back, and observe again the struggle, the dark time we have been coming through, and it looks totally different.

St Gregory of Nyssa, I think, was the first to use the metaphor of a cloud to describe that period, remembering how Moses went up through the cloud onto the top of Mount Sinai. This metaphor afterwards became a commonplace of the spiritual writers. What we have to struggle through is a dark cloud, a 'Cloud of Unknowing'. But the extraordinary thing about a dark cloud is that when you get above it and look back, it is radiant and shining. From the top of a mountain or from the air every cloud looks gold or fluffy white – you look down on it and think what a lovely comfortable thing it must be to sit on, but when we were inside it, all was dark and gloomy and depressing. It's quite exhilarating to see how the top surface of a cloud is always radiant. When Moses climbed Mount Sinai he came through a cloud. The people beneath saw only the lower edge of the cloud, dark and threatening. For Moses the experience on the way up must have been that of walking in damp thick fog. And then on the top of Mount Sinai, if he had bothered to look back – I am sure he had more important things at which to look forward – if he had bothered to look back he would have realised that all that darkness and gloom was simply the lower side of the radiance and the light.

The Cloud is not God's punishment: it is God's schooling, God's tuition. Coming through this time of darkness is the only way to the radiance, to the upper levels. We realise then, looking back on it, that, yes, we were not abandoned: we were never abandoned! God was there all the time, coaxing us on. And the profundity of the love of God as we reached the top of the mountain – now we see how glorious it is! We are glad now that we have come through the Cloud. All the time we were in the Cloud we kept trying to remember the time when we were in the plain: the time when we had been quite content to stay as we were in the lowland light. Now we have come to realise that if we had stayed down there we would never have found this new glory, never seen the top of the clouds.

Our Lord never lets us stagnate, always wants us to move on. The joy and the ebullience of the first fervour of our conversion is something that would get stale, if he left us in it for ever. It's not deep enough; it's not wide enough to satisfy us. We have to come through the Cloud into the greater glory. So we can sit on top of Mount Sinai, on top of Monte Gozo, or even Mount Carmel, and look back at the shining Cloud that had once been all mist and rain. It was the love of God that brought us through it. Now at last we can thank God for all those dreadful times, those months or even years that we've been blundering around in the darkness. We can thank him and praise him, and then we become somewhat abashed that we didn't appreciate the Cloud as much as we should have. We complained about it so much! Yet the Lord reassures that the whole point about coming through the Cloud is not to see where you're going. If we had understood what was going on we would not really have been in the Cloud of Unknowing. It's because we didn't understand, because we were in doubt and in real darkness that the Lord was able to lead us. If we had known where we were going, or if we thought we knew where we were going, we wouldn't have come out on the right side at all. For the darkness was the love of God. "Is my gloom, after all, Shade of His hand, outstretched caressingly?" The sheer fact that at the time we had found it so distressing, and that we took no pleasure in earthly things, proves that we had been really in love with God after all.

We come out into the radiance, into the sunlight. And the one thing we can be sure of is that whatever happens in the future we're never going to have to go back through that particular cloud again. God always leads us on. The path will have its ups and downs, and there will be darkness and light in the future, but every time it will be something different. Our Lord is always new, always fresh. We will never again have to experience precisely the difficulty we have come through. We'll never again feel precisely the first joys of our conversion. Everything has become different and renewed, more profound. And as the pilgrimage goes on – pilgrimages never really end – as we go on we have to go on climbing, spiralling upwards towards the Lord. The experience of darkness and the experience of light is different every time. Having come through it once we may have a bit of an idea of what to expect, but Our Lord is full of surprises....

When Mary Magdalene and the other women came to the garden they did not expect to do anything but mourn and grieve. It's just possible that one or two of them remembered the vague hints, the prophecies, 'lying in the bosom of the earth for three days and three nights'; but they wouldn't have expected one day and two nights! Our Lord's Resurrection would have come as a surprise even if some of them had remembered this prophecy, though all the indications in the Gospel are that none of them realised what he was talking about, none of them did expect him to rise. But then somehow there he is.

The Resurrection takes place so gently: they don't actually witness any of the dramatic events, the earthquake, the rolling away of the stone. They find an empty tomb and a young man dressed in white, a message of joy! It takes a long time before they realise that it's really true. Some of the women go running back ... there's a lot of confusion. All the Gospel writers have different versions, as if there was so much joy that no one was able actually to sit down systematically and write a diary of it. And years later when they were telling the story to the evangelists they all got rather muddled about the details. But they all agree that they didn't expect it. It took a long time for it to sink in. Gradually, one by one, they came to realise, yes, it is true, the Lord is truly risen. And they find him now changed: the same Lord, but changed. The risen body is not the same as the body that was born in Bethlehem: it's been transformed, glorified. Some of

the wounds are still visible, but they too have been transfigured. Perhaps Peter and James and John remember that glimpse they'd once seen of him transfigured, but for the others it must have been a surprise, a reawakening of their own faith, as they see the risen Christ.

They hardly recognised him at first. After all, most of them had only known him weather-beaten and worn after years of toil. They'd known him after he had been walking the lanes of Galilee and Judea for three years, unkempt, scarred, battered and sunburnt. Now suddenly they see him made new, his flesh transformed: no wrinkles, no stains, hardly recognisable! Some of them even walk with him a Sabbath day's journey before they know who he is. So very gently it is that Our Lord allows them to see the rebirth of joy in their lives. It would have been far too much to know it all of a sudden!

The Gospels tell us nothing about how Our Lady heard the news of the Resurrection, yet we know that she too must have been gradually brought to this realisation, gradually filled with joy and glory, seeing her Son again. Yes, this is the Son that she bore, the Son that she carried, nursed and looked after, and who afterwards looked after her; but now he is transformed and glorified, so that her love for him is something different, something deeper. So it was that the glory of the Resurrection was so great that Our Lady and the apostles came to understand that it had been necessary to pass through Calvary in order to see him risen.

Chapter Twelve

Together on High

Free from bonds of time and distance,
Lost to sight, but close above,
Each of us can now embrace him,
Clinging to his feet in love.

We came down Monte Gozo, hopped over the stream, and up the hill at last into the city of Santiago de Compostela. Through the walls we came, into the narrow streets, past the first market square and the second, round the back of the big enclosed Benedictine convent, and into the great Plaza del Obradoiro, the Place of the Work of Gold, dominated by the cathedral with its mighty flight of steps and its two massive towers, all 'work of gold'.

There we found the rest of our company, so we were all reunited. About ten minutes afterwards walked in a Frenchman, a sculptor, who had come alone on foot all the way from Tours with a dog at the end of a string. A little later a group of Germans arrived with a priest. We found that a great company of people was gathering from all over Europe, pilgrims to St James. We were given certificates by the Pilgrim Office – I've still got mine somewhere – declaring that we were entitled to call ourselves Pilgrims of Compostela and on certain occasions to wear a scallop shell. And so our own group was back together, and we found ourselves united with other people, from different backgrounds, different languages, different countries, all drawn together by the one pilgrimage.

The realisation that we are not just an accidental group but essentially a fellowship is part of what it means to be a Catholic. The Church is far more than just a random collection of people

who might be useful if we need some help on our way. The Church is actually the Body of Christ, the Temple of the Holy Spirit. Initially, in the first fervour of our conversion, we may have thought of the Church as no more than a jolly bunch of people to be with: "Here's a nice group of companions. We've all got our different skills and talents. We can help each other on our way. Isn't it nice that we've met!" But gradually, as our faith deepens and the glory of the Resurrection begins to work in our life, we realise that the Church is so much greater than that. The Church is the living Body of Christ. The Church is the means by which Christ lives in the world now. And we're not just an accidental assembly of people: we've been chosen, we've been called before the creation to be the Church, and we all have our part in it. We are members of something that is very much greater than the sum of its parts. "I believe in the Church," as the Creed says. (In the original Greek, the Creed of Nicea uses exactly the same preposition 'in' when it says we believe "*in* the Father, *in* the Son, *in* the Holy Spirit ... *in* the Church." In Greek, as in Latin, this carries much more weight than it does in English.)

We have to put our trust in the Church, which means accepting her whether we think she is a jolly bunch of people to be with or not. We can no longer say that the Church means no more than a collection of people helpful to be with, and that if we don't find them helpful to us, we can leave them and find somebody else. No, the Church is the one Body of Christ. And it is only in that realisation that our Catholic faith deepens; we become aware of how important it is for the Church to be One, to be One Body, one Unity; that if any members of the Church are lost, every member suffers; if any member of the Church falls into sin, we are all diminished; if any member of the Church leaves, wanders away, goes into schism or abandons the Faith, every one of us is diminished by that separation because we belong together. St Paul says, "If any part of the body is injured, the whole body feels pain," and so it is with the Church. We belong to each other.

We realise that the unity of the Church is not just something convenient for administration, not just something practical, or intended to impress people outside the Faith. The unity of the Church is of its very nature, and that is why the search for unity needs to be much more profound than I fear it is. Our unity must be a unity in the Body of Christ. We say "I believe in one Church," not in lots of churches. It's no good saying, "One sort of religion suits me and another sort of religion suits you, so let's have lots of different churches. As long they are all quite friendly with each other it doesn't really matter." I am afraid all too many people these days seem to think like that. I get the impression that very few are really concerned for the organic unity of the Church. Most seem to be quite happy to accept lots of different 'churches', lots of different ways of believing. As long as they are all vaguely friendly, as long as they can all share each other's communion, they don't want to go any closer into unity. And yet Our Lord is calling us into a much more profound, much deeper unity, so that we belong to each other, we belong together as one people, just as the children of Israel were called in the desert to be one people.

Israel was divided between the north and the south, and there was continual strife in the body of God's people, but it was the never-ending dream of the prophets, the saints of the Old Testament, to bring Israel back together. And so it is in the New Testament. Christendom has been sundered and divided and yet the one Church remains, essentially one and essentially together. Reunion can only mean a reunion into the One Body of Christ. Every division, every separation of Christians, diminishes every one of us. It's very sad that our age is characterised by many groups splitting off, new 'churches', new denominations being formed every year. There seems to be endless division. Each one of us is diminished by that.

On the other hand each one of us is benefited by all the good works of every member of the Church, and there are so very many. There are still martyrs and confessors, and the glory of the martyrs is not private to them alone. It's a glory for the whole Church when we hear of the suffering of Christians in Pakistan or Indonesia, or in other countries where there has been savage persecution. Every one of us has a share in that crown of martyred glory. We hear of places where the Church is growing and flourishing, and we hear of enormous increases in the Church in many parts of Africa, the Far East and particularly in Korea and the Philippines, even in China. The Church worldwide is growing and flourishing: more and more converts are coming to the Faith, and so we too are growing. We can rejoice in the success of the Church. We hear of countries where the Church has been set free after a period of persecution. In countries like Ukraine or Albania, where the persecutions are over, the Church has come out into the open, and it is revealed that the Faith has always been preserved, and God's people have increased and multiplied, and all the decades of persecution did nothing to dampen the Faith. And every one of us has a share in that glory, in that happiness. We belong together.

We belong together particularly because when times were difficult in certain parts of the Church, our prayers have been sustaining them. If we prayed for the conversion of Russia all those seventy years since Our Lady came to Fátima, we can really have a share in the joy as that conversion takes place. Certainly we can rejoice when we hear reports that well over half the population of Russia are devout practising Christians, a far higher proportion than in our own country. Perhaps now it's time we should ask them to pray for us! We pray for each other and we rejoice in each other's success. And we rejoice also in the martyrdom, in the glory of the saints, because it is characteristic of the martyrs that they go to their triumph rejoicing, glad that through their suffering the Church grows.

We belong to each other, so if we grieve with the parts of the Church that are failing, falling away, falling into sin, we can also rejoice with the parts that are growing. If we look at the Church throughout the world, there are more parts growing and flourishing than there are diminishing and falling away. The Body of Christ is one people and we belong together. We can feel that unity throughout the world. Sometimes there are occasions when we can see and join people gathered from many different countries, but we don't need to be physically present in one place to be one Church. We know that we are one people, one body in Christ because of our unity in the sacraments.

It is the will of Christ: he tells us that all his people should be one flock under one shepherd, and that's something which we continue to pray for. It's something which has never yet been fully granted to us. Since the very beginning, the time of the Acts of the Apostles, there have been divisions from the Church. People decided that they didn't really care about the Church, they only wanted to be together with their own special group: and so on one pretext or another a sect leaves the Church. The mistake they all make is to think that the only purpose of the Church is to be a nice group of people to be with, so that if we don't happen to like some of these people we may leave them and go off on our own. The whole point of being one Church is that we need the difficult people and the weak people. They need us: we need them. We can support them: they can pray for us. We belong together. Once we begin to go off and form special groups, apart from the Church, then the whole Church is diminished.

It was only in the first few days that the Church was really one and there were no dissident Christians of any sort (unless you count St Thomas for a week!), during the first forty days until Our Lord ascended into heaven. They came out from Jerusalem, and in the sight of the apostles he was caught up into heaven. His Ascension was not an act of going away: it was more a mode of being present. He was no longer confined to being just one body in one place at one time: he was free to be available, to be with us wherever we gather. He said, "Wherever two or three of you are gathered in my name, I am there in the midst of you." It is because of the Ascension that he becomes free of the whole of space and time, free to be with us here, free to be with us wherever the Church gathers. So the Church is formed in the presence of Christ. The presence of Christ is diffused into the world through his Ascension.

Immediately after the Ascension St Luke describes the Church for us: "They waited in Jerusalem, gathered around the eleven apostles, gathered in prayer around Mary, the mother of Jesus." That's our first ever definition of the Church, in the first chapter of the Acts of the Apostles: "The apostles gathered in prayer round Mary, mother of Jesus." If we are in doubt as to where the Church is – and there seem to be so many bodies claiming to be the Church – we need only look for the apostles gathered around Mary, the Mother of Jesus. That's why she's been called the Mother of the Church, because it is to her that the Church looks for a guarantee that we are on the right path, that we are one with her Son. She is the centre around which the apostles gathered. As long as we remain faithful to the apostles and to Mary, the mother of Jesus, then we are the Church. We are the Body of Christ We are really gathered in his name: he is really present among us.

Chapter Thirteen

An Abundance of Gifts

Fiery tongues and roar of tempest
Shake the house with joy and fear.
Mary and the Twelve are praying;
Gentle voice of calm they hear.

We had arrived in the holy city of Compostela, and it wasn't even raining, so there was a chance to explore the city. It is a very rugged stone-built sort of place, with covered passages alongside all the main streets, rather like Chester; lots of little old shops, selling books and rosaries, as well as toothpaste and tinned tuna. There were several old churches, and a lovely enclosed convent which we discovered near the cathedral. Unlike most Carmelite chapels, the benches for outsiders were between the grille and altar, so the sisters were behind us, usually with their curtains drawn. Hearing the Office being sung was very moving, as the sound of disembodied voices filtered through the curtain into the church.

There were a number of other impressive buildings. Flanking the cathedral are the bishop's house, the chancery and a hostel for pilgrims. In the great Plaza del Obradoiro was an enormous hostel which had been built by King Ferdinand and Queen Isabella for pilgrims, but Franco had turned it into a four-star hotel so real pilgrims couldn't afford to stay there any more. But they did keep up their old tradition of giving a meal to all pilgrims who arrived on foot, so we got our free meal. We found ourselves somewhere to stay that we could afford: a nice little one-star fonda called the Hostal Moure, 'hostel for Moors' – I thought Spanish devotion to St James was based on the idea that he drove the Moors out of

Spain! It was the first time for weeks that we'd had real rooms with real beds and real sheets. One of the symbols of St James, no one knows quite why, is the scallop. So the girls explored the fish market and managed to find some scallops which were then cooked for us by one of the boys on his terrifying little petrol stove. So we sat in our warm, dry, clean rooms in the fonda and we had our coquilles Saint-Jacques and we felt that good things were coming into our life again.

There are times when we realise that God does give us good things. Suddenly we seem to be filled with the gifts of the Holy Spirit, uncountable, beyond the neat calculations of the Catechism. We count up the seven gifts listed by Isaiah and the twelve fruits mentioned by St Paul, and still there is more: gifts, charisms, call them what you will. All we know is that the Holy Spirit is giving us good things in abundance. When the darkness lifts from our life of prayer we become aware again of the presence of God, as we rejoice in all the gifts which the Holy Spirit has given us, the good things that God has poured out on us. And then we realise, with a certain amount of embarrassment, that he had actually been pouring out all these gifts on us even during the dark period.

The Holy Spirit is not fickle. He comes into our life at Baptism. He is renewed in all the Sacraments, especially Confirmation. He goes on giving us the grace that we need: and there are so many different sorts of grace! I'm no theologian, but the real experts can distinguish some fifty different species of grace in their winter and summer plumage. The love of God comes in so many different forms. When we were first converted, or were first received, the Holy Spirit was liable to give us some of the more ebullient and exciting gifts, in the ardour of the joy of the Lord; the sort of thing that makes people jump up and down, clap their hands and sing! Later, as we mature in the faith, we find that he's giving us much deeper, more profound gifts. It means we can look back with some amusement at our first charisms: they seem like cherry blossom, light and airy but not very serious. Then the blossom fades and the tree looks rather dull: only later do the cherries come. It's a bit like that with the Holy Spirit. We had our time of blossom when everything was light and frivolous and happy. And then the blossom fell away and we thought everything had gone wrong, the Holy Spirit had let us down. What we didn't realise was that those hard, unattractive-looking green objects on the ends of the twigs would ripen and take colour, maturing into cherries. When our spiritual cherries finally do ripen, we realise that the power and the grace of God had been at work the whole time. In particular we see that the greatest gifts of the Holy Spirit – faith, hope and charity, these three – have never actually been missing. In those terrible dark periods when we felt that we didn't believe in anything, we kept going somehow: that was faith! In the same way, although we couldn't envisage ever coming through into a time of peace, somehow we kept going: that was hope. And there was love there as well.

The remarkable thing is that when we're feeling thoroughly depressed, dry and desolate, we feel that there is no joy, no grace in our life whatsoever, that is precisely the moment when somebody else looking at us may say, "What a marvellous example of faith, of love and hope we see here!" It can be very disconcerting just when we're feeling our worst and somebody comes up and says, "It's always nice being with you because you're such a radiant example of God's grace." We think, "Sorry, you've got the wrong address!" No, the Holy Spirit does keep working and the gifts do keep coming: we don't notice them but other people do. Certainly God does.

We're given that grace in the Sacraments. We can drive it away by sin, yes, but God will never take it away. What he takes away is simply our perception of it. We may think we have no grace, we have no gifts, the Holy Spirit's doing nothing for us. Yet in reality, perhaps precisely because we aren't thinking about it, not conscious of it, grace is working so much more powerfully. When we are liberated from the dark cloud we can begin again to feel the power of the Holy Spirit. And the Spirit is given to us in so many different ways. There's no one way we can name and claim as the best, because every way is the best way for someone: we all have our different function in the Church. Yes, we all have faith and hope and love, we all need them: but there are many other gifts, gifts that vary. St Paul mentions many of them, like understanding, or teaching, even administration, (one of the great gifts of the Holy Spirit), to say nothing of the gifts of healing, the gifts of languages or prophecy.

Some people who might need the gift of languages are terribly aware that they haven't got it. I knew one missionary priest who was longing for the gift of tongues but found himself quite unable to cope with the language of the country he was supposed to work in. Yet the people among whom he worked were very pleased indeed with him. They didn't in the least bit mind about his curious grammar: they could see the Holy Spirit working in his other gifts. My friend spent a lot of time worrying that he hadn't got the gift of languages when really the Holy Spirit was doing marvels through the gift of preaching.

One of the things the Spirit often gives us is the gift of really appreciating doctrine, appreciating the truths of the faith. When we are beginners it can be so very difficult to remember the whole Catechism, to try and work out what we're supposed to believe, and what we're supposed to do. A lot of it can seem very external to us. We can say, "Oh yes, the Church teaches this, that and t'other, and therefore we believe it," but we don't take it into ourselves. We will say, if we are asked, "Yes, of course, I accept the dual procession of the Holy Spirit and the hypostatic union," but it can seem no more than just words. Until the Holy Spirit really gets to work, and then it suddenly becomes real to us. We may not be familiar with the technical language, we still may get confused about transubstantiation and consubstantiation, but the truth behind the language suddenly becomes alive. We realise that the doctrines of the Church are not just abstract things worked out on paper to keep the theologians off the streets. The doctrines of the Church are messages from and about the lover of my soul! This is the truth about Jesus Christ! The more we feel ourselves filled with the love of Christ the more we want to know about him; the more glad we are to understand everything that the Spirit has told the Church. And so the doctrines of the Faith become tremendously exciting: indeed it at this stage of one's life it is a real grief to hear others say they are not important. When we see all these learned ecumenical theologians who don't seem to care tuppence about points of doctrine, we feel they're saying they don't care about the one we love more than anyone else. That can be a great cross to bear.

Other people may not have that realisation, but they have other gifts. One of the things we have to understand is how God chooses us right at the beginning, not through our merits but for his kind purposes. We can be filled with an understanding of the truth of doctrine. We can also be filled with an understanding of the moral teachings of our faith, why it is that we try to live in the sight of God in the way we try to do. All this is an enlightenment of the Holy Spirit which is for the building up, not just of our faith, but the faith of the whole Church. For that purpose also the Holy Spirit does occasionally give those embarrassing gifts of working miracles, which the saints always find so very difficult to cover up. Miracles are not rare in the Church but luckily there are ways of concealing them. Our Lord was always very anxious that people should not be swept off their feet by miracles. If he cured someone he usually said, "Don't tell everyone about it," meaning that it's not that important: the important thing is to love God. You find the same if you look at the lives of all the saints: they covered up their miracles and tried to get people to look at what was really important.

The miracles that we witness nowadays are most often associated with shrines and places of pilgrimage, or with the Sacraments, and we can easily see it's nothing to do with us:

it's the grace of the Holy Spirit. One of the great things about the Sacraments is that whatever grace, whatever power comes through them, (and it's amazing to see what does happen through the Sacraments), is very obviously the work of the Holy Spirit channelled through us, through the power of the whole Church. The Sacrament of Anointing is a tremendous prayer for healing, and it begins in the cathedral in Holy Week when the bishop and all the priests pray together over the oil: then each time we confer the sacrament the Holy Spirit can work through the oil of anointing for the healing of minds and souls and bodies.

The Holy Spirit comes to us very gently and yet with tremendous force and tremendous power. As the prophet Amos said, "If you hear a lion roaring, you can't help being afraid. If you hear the Lord calling you can't help but prophesy." The spirit of prophecy is something which is given to the Church again and again. Preaching and prophesying are really the same thing, speaking the word of the Lord, encouraging, rebuking if need be, urging on, spelling out the love of God to all those in need of it. Elijah was called in a very special way to be a prophet, to be the witness outside the community. His job was to make life uncomfortable, to remind people of the truth: rather as Socrates called himself the 'gadfly of Athens', so Elijah was the 'troubler of Israel'. He was the one who stopped Israel being fat and complacent and sleek and sitting back and enjoying life, forgetting about the Lord. Elijah was needed again and again to remind the people of Israel of the word of the Lord. So it is in the Church that again and again the Lord raises up prophets. Sometimes they are outside the community like Elijah, and the prophet must witness by withdrawing from the rest of society, the rest of the Church, speaking in words of silence, symbolic actions and gestures, or at other times in writing, and always by prayer. Others have the task of being witnesses within the community, living among the people, like Elisha. Certainly the Church has never lacked prophets of that sort. There are many priests, religious and lay people who have this function of prophet today.

The Spirit is never taken back. God does not withdraw his grace, but as we go through life different gifts emerge, different ones mature. We realise that the first things the Spirit gave us when we were young have served their purpose, and now the time has come for deeper and more profound gifts that the Spirit gives us as life goes on. The life of the Spirit never comes to an end. And of these gifts faith, hope and love endure, because without them we couldn't persevere at all. Faith, hope and love are never withdrawn, even in our times of greatest darkness. We may not see them but they are there.

When the Spirit came on Pentecost Sunday he came to confirm in the lives of the apostles and Our Lady the gifts and the graces that had already been given. Our Lady was overshadowed by the Holy Spirit at the Annunciation. The apostles had seen the Spirit coming down in the Jordan at Baptism, and more than once Our Lord had given them the Holy Spirit. When he met them after his Resurrection he breathed on them and said, "Receive the Holy Spirit." They had already been filled with the Holy Spirit, but what happened on Pentecost was that they become aware of this. They become aware that they had never lost the gift of the grace of the Spirit that was poured out on them from the beginning. Even in those dark days during the trial, the suffering and passion of Our Lord, the Holy Spirit had never been withdrawn. Faith, hope and love had stayed with them. Even in the time of confusion after the Ascension, when they were unsure what to do, they were frightened and they gathered round Mary for comfort, even then the gifts of the Spirit were with them. Suddenly at Pentecost there's a great surge of relief as they become aware of the power of the Spirit, aware then of other gifts, of other good things the Lord is pouring out on them for the building up of the Church. Immediately after receiving that grace of the Spirit, the apostle Peter turns round to throw open the windows, and comes out on to the balcony to preach to the crowd, bringing the message of

God to thousands of people on that first day.

Our Lady also was there at Pentecost. She might have thought that her task was over, and yet she too was given the grace of the Holy Spirit. It seems certain that she remained with the apostles, particularly with St John, and for some period after the coming of the Holy Spirit at Pentecost she was with them, still full of grace, still overshadowed by the Holy Spirit, giving them comfort and consolation and strength at the beginning of the Christian mission.

Chapter Fourteen

Word made Flesh

Hail! a woman wrapped in glory,
Moon and stars and sun enfold.
Caught up by her Son's redemption,
Soul and body safe and whole.

The goal of our pilgrimage was of course the cathedral church of Santiago de Compostela. The outside of the cathedral all looks very eighteenth century, very elaborate, very baroque, with its two towers of honey-coloured stone glistening in the sun. But inside, sheltered by the baroque work, is the old twelfth-century entrance, carved all over in the most intricate of designs. In the middle is a statue of St James, and at its feet a place where so many pilgrims have put their hands that it has worn into the shape of a hand. Inside is a long Romanesque church with later ornamentation. The Spanish like decorating their churches with enormous complexity, so above the altar and around the sanctuary are endless statues and carvings of angels and saints. I think we counted at least six images of St James in the sanctuary alone.

In the centre of the church hangs the biggest thurible in the world, the *botafumeiro*. It stands about shoulder high when it's on the ground: they haul it up on ropes and swing it across from one transept of the church to the other. It is a very impressive sight, but most distracting all through Mass. High above the altar is the oldest statue of all, an image of St James which is so encrusted with jewels and additions that nobody knows quite how old it is. The tradition is that you end your pilgrimage by climbing up a narrow flight of steps above the altar to embrace the statue from behind. There's a continual procession of people clambering up to embrace it, and then down on the other side. The statue itself is not particularly beautiful, though you can't really tell what shape it is under all its encrustations, but to climb up and cuddle it serves as a silent act of homage to St James, a prayer in action.

Underneath the statue is the high altar, and underneath that is a secret little chapel: we managed to get permission to say Mass there. In the chapel is the body of St James in a long silver coffin. The body was only found about a hundred years ago, after being lost for centuries, but they were able to prove it was the original one by comparing it with a relic in England. This had been cut off by order of King Henry III and enshrined in Reading Abbey. It somehow survived the fall of the Abbey and is now in the Catholic Church at Great Marlow. This relic was found to fit exactly onto the body found in Compostela a hundred years ago, so we can be sure that the body now preserved is the same one venerated in the Middle Ages. There is of course a gap of some seven or eight hundred years between the mediæval shrine and the time of the apostles, so whether it is really the body of St James is known only to the angels, but there it is, and people have prayed at that place for at least a thousand years.

The chapel is so small that there is there is no possibility of having an altar facing the people: there just isn't room. The eight of us had to stand side by side, and that filled the chapel. There was no room even for anyone to stand behind me: we all had to stand side-by-side together before the altar. That was the first time that it struck me how placing the altar between priest and people can be a real barrier, and how much more it means for us all to be facing the same way, all equal before God and St James. We felt very much at one during that Mass, and in our Mass of course we received Holy Communion. So above the body of St James we found the Body of Christ. By partaking the Body of Christ we became the Body of Christ.

Now the history of the body of St James may be obscure, but there is one fact which is certain. It is the most important fact in the whole of world history: that the Word was made Flesh. God became a man, a human being like us, body and soul. We say in the Creed "He was made man" and we bow; we used to read the Gospel passage "The Word was made flesh" at the end of every Mass. Although we repeat those words so often in our Christian tradition, we don't always live as if we believed it. Because what we're saying is that this material creation of God has been sanctified and united to God. The old puritanical idea is not dead, that material creation is somehow evil, that only the spirit is of any importance – but can we forget that the Word became flesh!

This earth that God created has been made holy. It was of course made holy in the very act of creation, but then it was damaged and corrupted by sin, though not totally destroyed. Perhaps that's where the Puritans go wrong. Many of our modern Puritans tell us that because of sin this world and everything in it was totally corrupted and there is nothing of holiness left in the world. The phrase is sometimes used that "The whole human race lies under God's dreadful wrath and condemnation." That's not the Catholic faith: we believe that the whole human race lies under God's dread love, the love of God that was made manifest when the Word was made flesh. This damaged creation of ours has been redeemed and then sanctified by the Holy Spirit, the Spirit that comes to renew the face of the earth – not just the face of the heavens, the face of the earth! But despite that, the old Manichæan heresy, the idea that matter is somehow evil, still lingers on. It shows itself in the various puritanical movements there have been even inside the Church. When they deny that there is any goodness in God's creation, that is as much to say that not only the creation but the redemption and the sanctification all went for nothing.

We believe the Word was made flesh, and that our human nature, our human world, the material world that we live in, was made holy. Because it was made holy it can serve as the vehicle of our worship. That's why the Catholic tradition has always been to use material things in our worship, and to use the very best we have. We build fine churches, elaborate altars of worked stone, carved as beautifully as we know how; we use sacred vessels of precious metal, adorned, made as beautiful as we can. We use vestments of the finest brocade all set about with embroidery. In the Middle Ages, in the great ages of faith, no expense was spared in decorating the altar, for everything had to be of the very best, the finest that could possibly be made. Even the smallest poor country church would contain half the wealth of the parish, dedicated to the service of the altar, because here God's material creation is being used in the worship of God. The sad Puritans failed to see this and they took away all the beauty of worship. In the puritanical movement that swept through the Catholic Church forty years ago, so many of our churches were stripped of anything that was beautiful. They didn't realise it of course, but their work of destruction was effectively a denial that the Word was made Flesh.

God comes to us through the beautiful things he has made, through the beautiful things of natural creation, through the flowers, the birds and the animals. That is why we have an obligation to look after them. It's precisely because the world which God has made and given to us has been made holy, and sanctified by the Holy Spirit, that we have a duty to care for it, not to misuse it. The sad waste of God's creation is a blasphemy against the Holy Spirit. The beauties of nature, the animals, the birds, the sun and the moon, every created thing was formed by God for his honour and glory and for our use, even for our entertainment. Certainly some of the creatures seem to have been made chiefly for our amusement, and in the Psalms we hear that the Lord made the sea monsters to play with. We should appreciate that. We should never deny the beauty of God's creation. It's precisely because it's so holy that it needs to be treated with such care and such respect. It's because everything God has made was created good. The damage caused by sin was redeemed by Christ on the

Cross. The Holy Spirit sanctifies the face of the earth, so we have a special duty to care for this material creation, to care also for our own bodies, as well as our own souls.

We were made in the image and likeness of God. God comes to us in physical, solid, material things, and these things can be made holy and touched by God. That touch of God can be passed on through those things which he has touched. That's why we use holy water and blessed candles. That's why the sacred vessels of the altar are treated with great respect, or they should be – alas in some parishes they no longer are. But all these sacred things, the altar stone, the church building itself, the relics of the saints, are touched by God just as in the Old Testament we read that the bones of the prophet Elisha were a vehicle of God's grace and worked miracles. The prophet Haggai tells us that if you are carrying holy food in the fold of your garment everything you touch becomes holy. In the New Testament the napkins and towels used by St Paul were tokens of God's grace, so the people sought after them and used them in prayer. A woman was cured just by touching the fringe of Our Lord's cloak. God does use these material things and it has always been a sound Catholic instinct to revere the things God has created for the purposes of his worship.

Beyond these 'sacramentals' there are of course the Sacraments themselves. God comes to us from the touch of oil and the flowing of water and above all under the forms of bread and wine. And it is not just a 'spiritual' presence. Again the puritans fall into the error of saying that there is nothing at all in the material things: "They're only bread and wine. It's just in the act of eating and drinking that we somehow share in the presence of Christ." But no, Jesus tells us, "Truly, truly, I say to you, my flesh is real food. My blood is real drink." It is not just a spiritual symbolic presence. Christ is really given to us. We can touch him. St John Vianney used to say, "It's amazing, I can pick him up. I can carry him across here and he moves. I can carry him across there and he moves." (That isn't of course quite true. When we are carrying the Blessed Sacrament it's the world that moves under us; Christ stays still!)

Christ is given to us in a real, solid, physical, tangible form. That is because it's only physical things that we can be sure of. We can actually see the Blessed Sacrament: we can see the Host, we can feel it break. We can touch and taste. There is something we can be certain of. If our religion was purely spiritual, we'd never really know whether we'd received grace or not. If all we could do was to say, "I may or may not have had an illuminating experience of the Holy Spirit this morning when sharing bread and wine with my friends, but I can't really be sure whether it was genuine or not," we could never be sure that God loves us. When we say with assurance, "I have received the Body of Christ in the form of bread and wine," this is something we can be confident about. That is why God does speak to us in physical, solid matter, real stuff, because he created the heavens and the earth and saw that they were good. And God promised in the Resurrection not only a new heaven but a new earth as well: somehow this material creation is to be caught up in the glory of the Resurrection.

We can consider that all the beautiful things that have ever existed in the world and have been destroyed will be renewed at the Resurrection. I remember looking round the sad ruins of St Andrews Cathedral in Scotland with a friend who surprised me by saying, "How good it will be to see this cathedral restored on the Last Day." He was right, we shall, because anything that was beautiful in this world can't be totally lost. It's all held in being in the mind of Christ. Francis Thompson said something similar: "All which thy child's mistake fancies as lost, I have stored for thee at home." It is because of this sanctity of matter that even the bodies of the saints are treated as holy things. It means that the dear old Brother Ass which we spend so much of our life trying to keep under control, that same Brother Ass is the vehicle on which Jesus rides into Jerusalem! That's why the physical body which the saints sometimes appeared to treat with disrespect, the body that was tamed by fasting, by vigils, by scourging, that body is now enshrined in silver. The relics of the saints are kept as the most precious possessions of the Church because this is the Brother Ass which Our Lord rode into Jerusalem. Remember how St Teresa was pulled to pieces for relics almost before she died! Relics are kept and preserved because they are not just reminders of God's grace but actual vehicles of it. That's why we place relics in the altar and why we kiss the altar during Mass.

The Spirit renews the whole of creation, mind and body and soul, the birds and flowers and the trees and mountains, brother sun and sister moon. All of these are of God's creation, part of Christ's redemption. That's why Our Lady was assumed into heaven body and soul. Her body was not left to decay but was assumed into heaven to show that even when she grew old, the physical body in which she bore Our Lord remained a holy thing, so holy that it's caught up into heaven in anticipation. Our Lady was assumed into heaven just as Elijah, Moses and Enoch had been assumed. They were the few set aside from the whole of the Old Testament as forerunners, and Our Lady in a much more special way was chosen, to live already completely redeemed in heaven. For the rest of us there is a wait, a separation, as there was for those before Christ.

I once came across an unpublished sermon in a manuscript bundle of sermons by St John Chrysostom: not genuine, I'm afraid, but quite old nonetheless. It talks about the evening after the Crucifixion: the scene is set in Paradise, where Enoch and Moses and Elijah are talking together, having had heaven to themselves for several hundred years. Suddenly, to their dismay, a thief turns up. And they ask him, "What do you think you're doing here?" And the thief replies, "Well, if you're shocked to see me, you just wait: there'll be plenty more arriving tomorrow!"

Heaven is a place for bodies as well as souls. Heaven is the perfection of human nature and Our Lady is there as a forerunner for us. We have to suffer death and dissolution, the penalty of sin. Our Lady, who knew no sin, did not know decay, so she is perfected already. Yet she is only there to prepare a way for us. The glory of heaven and the resurrection of the body will include the renewal of the whole of our creation.

Chapter Fifteen

Well at the World's End

Crowned in heaven, Queen of angels,
Queen of saints, our Queen, our love;
Mary, show us how to listen,
How to follow Christ above!

Our Mass of Saint James was really the end of our pilgrimage. In theory we should have gone on to the Well at the World's End, on the coast at Finisterre, but we had run out of time and energy. All we could manage was to get the train back to Santander and the boat to Plymouth. I came back with a strong feeling that, whatever grace we'd gained or whatever indulgences we had won, we had definitely earned them! It was hard work, but the grace we gained was for a purpose. I felt I had a work to do in England. I'm still not quite clear what the work is in particular, but in general the purpose can only be the building up of God's Church.

That after all is really the only purpose of going on pilgrimage: to allow the grace of God to come into our lives for his purposes. There can be a dangerous tendency to concentrate on saving our own souls, and forget about other people's. I remember long ago hearing a monk preaching on vocations to us schoolboys: he said that when he first applied to join the monastery the abbot asked, "What have you come here for?" and he said, "To save my soul." Even at the time that seemed a bit odd to me. I came to understand later that the Lord has purposes deeper, more profound than just our own salvation. He wants us to work for the salvation of the world. God so loved the world that he sent his only Son, not to condemn the world but so that through him the world might be saved. Of course we must never be indifferent to our own salvation: that was the error of the Quietists four hundred years ago. We must not affect to despise our own chances of heaven. That would be a blasphemous rejection of God's love for us! Our desire must be to do God's will, and we know that part of God's will is our own salvation, but God's will also extends to the sanctification of the whole world.

St Paul tells us that God's will is for all to be saved. The Spirit comes to renew the face of the whole earth. We are to be God's instruments in that work of salvation. That's what being the Church means. We are all called into the Church, all in our very different ways. Our little group that went to Compostela were all very different, and all of us will, I hope, go on serving the Church in very different ways. St Paul points out that we do all need each other, we are all needed, for the upbuilding of the Church. There is so much still to be done! Our Lord came two thousand years ago to save the world, and he still calls us to be the Church, his body, his presence in the world, to continue that work of saving the world. That's why all the graces that are given to us in prayer, all the gifts that the Holy Spirit has already poured into us, are there for us to use for God's purposes. He never allows us just to enjoy grace for its own sake. We can never sit back and think, "At least I know that I am saved; I needn't bother about anybody else." There have been strange religions and odd aberrations that have taught people to think like that, but that's not what God offers. He offers us a share in his work of salvation, in his work of renewing all creation. That is why when God does give great graces of prayer they are never incompatible with a deep love of other people and a power to serve them in this world.

Superficial people outside may think that contemplative prayer is about denying the world altogether, hating the world and running away from it. It's not like that at all, is it? If we withdraw from the world, it's only in order to pray for it more effectively. One of the noticeable things about the saints is how very practical they are, how very loving. More especially, the higher they get in the realms of prayer and the closer they get to the mystical union with Our Lord, the more able they are to help other people. Think of St Thérèse of Lisieux, so deeply concerned with the needs of people. There was her childhood concern for the convict who was due to be executed: Thérèse took him on in her prayers, and managed to get him converted at the last minute. And then she took on the foreign missions: it's an indication of the mind of the Church that St Thérèse of Lisieux is the patron saint of the missions. You might have suggested as patron St Francis Xavier, or St Peter Claver, someone who actually went out and did it; but those who work on the foreign missions know perfectly well that without the prayers of the nuns at home they would never get anywhere. And then you have the big St Teresa, and St John of the Cross: great mystics, but also extremely practical people. We are told that one day St Teresa was caught in the kitchen having an ecstasy, floating gently off the floor with her face radiant, but continuing to fry the fish without burning them! The heights of mystical prayer don't take us away from the service of other people. They make us more available. St John of the Cross, I seem to remember, turned out to have a great talent for hydraulic engineering and all sorts of practical things.

Building up the Church needs the contemplative as well as the active vocation. Those of us who have been out in the mission-field of parish work know that it would all come to nothing without the praying sisters. Some people are called to go out to strange places and be heroically active. One thinks of all those who have gone off into South America and Africa and Asia to bring the Gospel, and the tremendous work that was done over the last hundred years, particularly in Africa where people were formed in a solid tradition of prayer. The real missionaries all began with a formation in prayer. They went out into the missions and they worked extremely hard and they founded churches, and now from those churches in Africa the missionaries are beginning to come back into Europe to re-convert us, because God knows that we do need it!

The work of the Church is a continual mutual giving from one side to the other. Some areas of the Church are rich in money and poor in faith. Others are the other way round, and we help each other. Whatever grace God gives us is meant to overflow. Our Lord says that we are to be "Measures pressed down, filled up and running over." The grace of God is something that should continually overflow in our lives. The Holy Spirit never stops pouring out gifts, and we must never stop letting them pass on from us. The grace of God has to flow through us. The love of God and the Faith are things which we can never totally give away. As fast as we try to give them away our hearts fill up again, so that we become, as the prophet said, 'fountains of living water'. We don't need to make leaky cisterns for ourselves. We can let the grace of God flow through us to build up his Church.

There's still a long way to go, there's still a lot of work to be done. We've been at it for two thousand years and still so many souls are unaware of the love of God. There is a great work to be done, in England and throughout the world. When Our Lady was assumed into heaven you might have thought – she might have thought – her work was done at last. Finally grace is perfected in her; she is already body and soul in heaven – but no, her work has hardly begun. She is crowned Queen of Heaven. That's not an empty title. She's no mere constitutional monarch. Her task as Queen of Heaven is to continue to direct the work of heaven on earth, and she has taken on this role of Mother, that she accepted at the foot of the Cross, to be the Mother of the Church. So she has continued to guide the Church ever since.

It is remarkable how Our Lady has worked and has been seen to work in so many places, so many times. I don't suppose there's a country in the world where there isn't a story of her appearing. Certainly there has been no century without stories of Our Lady coming, guiding, calling people. The message again and again is to repent, to believe in the Gospel. At Lourdes, at Fátima, everywhere, the message is the same: "Turn back to God; turn away from sin; believe in the Gospel; repent!" So the work of Our Lady was really only just beginning when she was crowned Queen of Heaven, and her work is due to continue till all is well at the World's End.